There is too much touristy sightseeing in the world these days, and not enough pilgrimage—intentionally joining and being joined by Jesus and his companions in daily discipleship. In his conversations, prayers, and reflections while walking on the old pilgrim trail to Canterbury, Nelson Kraybill makes pilgrims of us all.

—*Eugene H. Peterson, Professor Emeritus of Spiritual Theology, Regent College, Vancouver, B.C.*

Nelson Kraybill has a way with words, matching the elegant simplicity of the Pilgrims' Way. I relished every word of this book and often thought of biblical journeys, of John Bunyan's *Pilgrim's Progress*, of Chaucer's *Canterbury Tales*, of the film *Babette's Feast*, and of other stirring tales, including *Martyrs Mirror*. This book goes on my shelf with those classic tales of longing for God. I look forward to using *On the Pilgrims' Way* in the course I teach at Goshen College, "The Literature of Spiritual Reflection and Social Action." The class can go on this spiritual pilgrimage with Nelson and explore Jesus' call, "Follow me."

—*Shirley Hershey Showalter, President, Goshen College, Goshen, Indiana*

As one of the pilgrimage partners for this book, I didn't anticipate the misery of unremitting rain and the pain of feet sodden in a whole day's walk. Neither could I have predicted the intense relief and comfort of sharing hot drink, fresh bread, and rest at our lunchtime inn. These hikers' experiences pose vivid parallels both to uncertainties of the Christian way and to delights of communion with fellow travelers and with the Lord.

Nelson Kraybill reminds us that the joy of the Christian journey is that we don't travel this way alone. We go together as a pilgrim band, fitting our feet into the steps of our Master. Pilgrims' conversation truly is "a seedbed for growing faith" (page 16). As you read this book, you will overhear and want to join in such fertile talk.

Just reading the chapter titles entices one into this volume: risking, doubting, feasting, choosing, valuing, taking courage—these are signposts pointing the Christian pilgrims' way. If you are new to Christian faith, this book will help you chart the way ahead. If you are an experienced hiker or a weary walker, it will confirm the past and give you courage to carry on.

—*Eleanor Kreider, Regents Park College, Oxford, England*

On the Pilgrims' Way

Conversations on Christian Discipleship

J. Nelson Kraybill

Herald
Press

Scottdale, Pennsylvania
Waterloo, Ontario

Library of Congress Cataloging-in-Publication Data
Kraybill, J. Nelson.
   On the pilgrims' way : conversations on Christian discipleship /
J. Nelson Kraybill.
     p. cm.
   Includes bibliographical references.
   ISBN 0-8361-9097-1 (pbk. : alk. paper)
   1. Christian life.   2. Christian pilgrims and pilgrimages—England.
3. Kraybill, J. Nelson—Journeys—England. 4. England—Description and
travel.   I. Title.
   BV4501.2.K695   1999
   263'.04242—dc21   98-40632

The paper used in this publication is recycled and meets the minimum re-
quirements of the American National Standard for Information Sciences—
Permanence of Paper for Printed Library Materials, ANSI Z39.48-1984.

Scripture is used by permission, all rights reserved, and unless otherwise
identified is from the *New Revised Standard Version Bible,* copyright 1989
by the Division of Christian Education of the National Council of the
Churches of Christ in the USA; KJV, from *The Holy Bible, King James Version;* NCV, from *The Holy Bible, New Century Version,* copyright © 1987,
1988, 1991 by Word Publishing, Dallas, Texas 75039; REB, from *The Revised English Bible,* Cambridge Univ. Press, U.K.

The scallop shell on the cover is a traditional symbol of pilgrimage
(see page 15).

ON THE PILGRIMS' WAY
Copyright © 1999 by Herald Press, Scottdale, Pa. 15683
   Published simultaneously in Canada by Herald Press,
   Waterloo, Ont. N2L 6H7. All rights reserved
   Website for Herald Press: www.mph.org
Library of Congress Catalog Card Number: 98-40632
International Standard Book Number: 0-8361-9097-1
Printed in the United States of America
Book design by Gwen M. Stamm

08 07 06 05 04 03 02 01 00 99 10 9 8 7 6 5 4 3 2 1

To my daughter Laura,
baptized on December 14, 1997.
May you know joy and life
in your walk with Jesus.

Contents

Preface

Writing a book should not be as enjoyable as this one was to produce! When Herald Press invited me to draft a small volume on Christian discipleship, I don't think they had in mind the diary of a pilgrimage. The book was supposed to be a guide for new Christians and others seeking to know God more fully; it was to be written from an Anabaptist perspective.

My full work schedule and good intentions to write a book did not at first produce results. Then I struck upon the idea of combining several experiences I have found life-giving: prayer, Bible study, silence, conversation with friends, and walking in ✳ the English countryside.

What emerged was a pilgrimage, during which I heard the wisdom of disciples from several Christian traditions—Anglican, Catholic, Baptist, Methodist, Bruderhof, independent, and Mennonite. From these fellow believers, I drew what seemed most helpful for those seeking to know and follow Jesus. This search has always been the central concern of the Anabaptist movement.

I thank the following people, who read an early draft of this book and made valuable suggestions that improved its quality and usefulness: Janeen Bertsche Johnson, Ted Koontz, Eleanor Kreider, Alan Kreider, Alice Roth, Myron Augsburger, Ellen Kraybill, and David Garber. I also thank each of my fellow pilgrims, who read the chapters pertaining to their respective parts of the journey and made helpful comments.

Mennonite Board of Missions (Elkhart, Indiana), which supported my family and me during our years in England, financed

7

the modest cost of this project. I am pleased that firstfruit royalties from this book will benefit the same organization, which has been so effective in sharing the good news of Jesus around the world.

—*J. Nelson Kraybill, President*
Associated Mennonite Biblical Seminary
Elkhart, Indiana

A Pilgrim Psalm

My soul longs, indeed it faints for the courts of the Lord;
my heart and my flesh sing for joy to the living God.
Even the sparrow finds a home,
and the swallow a nest for herself,
where she may lay her young, at your altars,
O Lord of hosts, my King and my God.
Happy are those who live in your house,
ever singing your praise.
Happy are those whose strength is in you,
in whose heart are the highways to Zion.

—Psalm 84:2-5

Taking a Pilgrimage

Across southern England, in gently rolling hills of the North Downs, there stretches an ancient trackway where Christians have walked for centuries as part of their longing for God. This chalkstone pathway once carried multitudes of pilgrims to the magnificent cathedral at Canterbury, after an event happened there in 1170 that shocked all of Europe. *1162*

The bishop of Canterbury, Thomas Becket, dared to disagree with the king of England. Knights loyal to the king challenged the bishop, followed him into the cathedral, and murdered him there. Within days people began making journeys to Canterbury to see Becket's tomb and honor his memory. There were reports of healings and miraculous events connected with the tomb. In the next centuries, millions came from Britain and all of Europe to pray at Becket's shrine inside Canterbury cathedral.

One of the great pieces of medieval literature is *Canterbury Tales,* by Geoffrey Chaucer. It still delights modern readers with earthy and entertaining stories that pilgrims told to each other on their way to Becket's tomb. In 1538 Henry VIII tried to stop the English practice of making pilgrimages. Yet centuries later people still know that the ancient road across southern England once guided thousands to Canterbury. Today people call that footpath the Pilgrims' Way.

By happenstance of history, much of the Pilgrims' Way has not been turned into a modern highway. It was too far up the hillsides. Instead, roads were built from village to village in valleys below. At a few places, the old Pilgrims' Way goes through an unpleasant stretch of industrial development or has been

The Pilgrims' Way often is worn deep into the landscape by centuries of travelers.

turned into a modern highway. In those stretches, a modern footpath called the North Downs Way runs closely parallel. Today's ramblers can walk from Winchester to Canterbury, most of the way through meadow and wood, across windswept hilltops and rain-spattered downs.

A Long Tradition of Spiritual Journey

There is a long tradition of God's people making literal step-by-step journeys to places of spiritual significance. Psalm 84 records prayers and comments of a pilgrim going to worship in the temple at Jerusalem: "My soul longs, indeed it faints for the courts of the Lord; my heart and my flesh sing for joy to the living God" (Psalm 84:2). I have often identified with the combination of longing and rejoicing reflected in that psalm.

Jesus knew something about pilgrimage. The earliest biblical story we have of Jesus, after his infancy, is when at age twelve he made a pilgrimage to Jerusalem with his parents. Many years later, near the end of his teaching and healing ministry, once again "his face was set toward Jerusalem" (Luke 9:53). That was a costly journey through betrayal and crucifixion. But Jesus' faithfulness opened up the possibility of new life for all of humankind.

In my years of seeking to know and follow Jesus, I have come to understand that Christian discipleship is not just a one-time commitment. Instead it is a daily process of arriving at crossroads and making decisions. Being a Christian is more like *going* somewhere than having arrived, more like being on a pilgrimage than in a sheltered haven. Pilgrims are people who disregard the "normal" priorities of life, who expect to meet God as they travel toward a destination of hope and life. Day after day, they face obstacles, nurse blisters, and experience the deep joy of being on a journey that nurtures the soul.

Today God may call you and me to leave our present physical or spiritual place and "head off to Jerusalem." Sometimes God calls us to leave an attachment to things (such as career, bank account, or house). Sometimes when God's Spirit summons, we move to a distant place.

Our walk with Jesus is a pilgrimage, a step-by-step journey in which we get a foretaste of the joy and restored relationships that someday will cover the earth in the kingdom of God. This kingdom is not so much a place as it is a people who accept the reign of God. It is a new society of people from many races and nations who live in the freedom of obedience to God. This people is "called to belong to Jesus Christ" (Romans 1:6).

A Modern Pilgrimage

At the age of forty-one, after five years of living in London, I set aside twelve days to be with Jesus in a way that pressures of daily life do not permit. I wanted to step back for a while from my work schedule to have uninterrupted days of prayer, Bible study, conversation, and silence. Because I love the English countryside, and often have found nurture for body and soul in walking the hills of Britain, I decided to do my reflection while walking the Pilgrims' Way.

I didn't want to make this pilgrimage entirely alone. During the five years I lived in England, I learned to know Christians from a variety of traditions. They taught me much about Christian discipleship. So I planned a twelve-day itinerary, chose topics and Bible passages for each day, and invited one or more fellow pilgrims to join me for each day of the journey. Without exception every person I asked took a day out of their own busy schedules, met me at a train station along the route, and shared a day of fellowship on the road.

What follows is an account of that journey, with notes from conversations and events along the way. Many people over the years have encouraged me with their insights on following Jesus. Similarly, I hope that my walk on the Pilgrims' Way might be useful to others.

I carried a notebook in my rucksack and strapped a camera on my belt, to record what I saw and learned. I often took notes while walking, even in the rain. I asked questions of my fellow pilgrims and listened to their stories. My wife, Ellen, walked with me on two occasions, once with our daughters Laura (13) and Andrea (8). During most days I had company. Most evenings I was alone, either at an inn or at a bed-and-breakfast.

Walking every day, in a linear route toward a distant destination, is different from taking an occasional circular hike in the countryside. "Pilgrim" became my identity, and I soon felt different from the people I met in villages and inns. My purpose was to seek God and to learn the seasoned wisdom of other seekers. I wanted to have a different identity.

I fostered the sense of alternative purpose by never using any means of transportation other than my two feet. Even when lodging was two miles off the footpath at the weary end of a day, I walked to my place of rest. The slower pace and physical limitations gave an intimacy with the countryside that I never experienced before.

Each day I focused on a selection of verses from the book of Psalms and from the Gospel of Luke. It was easy to decide on the Psalms, for it is the songbook of ancient Israel and should be a regular part of any Christian's life. Choosing Luke was more ar-

The scallop shell is a traditional symbol of pilgrimage, once worn as a badge by pilgrims returning from the Holy Land.

bitrary, since there are four such accounts of Jesus' ministry in the New Testament. Any of the four could have served well.

I chose Luke because the author is particularly alert to the way Jesus' ministry made an impact on wider society. I also favored Luke because it is the only Gospel that includes a sequel— Acts, the story of the early church in the years after Jesus' resurrection.

Meeting Jesus on the Road

The Gospel of Luke tells a remarkable story of what happened along the road from Jerusalem to Emmaus on the Sunday after Jesus died. Two disciples of Jesus, overwhelmed by grief from loss of their Lord, did not realize that the stranger who fell into step beside them was Jesus himself:

> *As they came near the village to which they were going, he walked ahead as if he were going on. But they urged him strongly, saying, "Stay with us, because it is almost evening and the day is now nearly over." So he went in to stay with them. When he was at the table with them, he took bread, blessed and broke it, and gave it to them. Then their eyes were opened, and they recognized him; and he vanished from their sight. They said to each other, "Were not our hearts burning within us while he was talking to us on the road, while he was opening the scriptures to us?"*
> *(Luke 24:28-32)*

Even before they knew it was Jesus, their hearts were "burning" within them as they discussed the Scriptures and talked about what had just happened in Jerusalem. I also had that experience, meeting our Lord in the faith and love of old friends and new acquaintances who spent a day with me on the Pilgrims' Way or broke bread at an inn along the way. My heart burned within me. Conversation is an excellent seedbed for growing faith. I have learned the value of comparing notes with fellow pilgrims on this unpredictable, demanding, and exhilarating pilgrimage of the kingdom of God.

Using This Book

Because I could not fully anticipate what would happen each day, or what fellow pilgrims would teach me, there is a certain haphazard character to this book. I tried to assign overall themes to each day, but often they became sidetracked by the flow of events and conversation. What follows is a narrative record of living experience, not the organized structures of systematic theology. I hope interweaving themes and repeating patterns of the story will create a provocative and useful picture of Christian discipleship.

There are several ways to use this book. It can be read straight through as a travelogue, or in sections as a stimulus to careful reflection. At the end of each chapter is a prayer and a list of questions for reflection. These questions might work for group discussion, or as topics for a personal journal.

I hope this book may inspire others to make an actual pilgrimage of their own, to discover the delight and exhaustion of many days on foot on a spiritual quest. Most of all, I hope that this record of one pilgrimage will encourage others to know and follow Jesus with joy and courage.

Do Not Be Afraid

Friday, May 17
Getting started in London and Farnham

Many pressures draw us away from following Jesus • We have to make a choice in response to Jesus' invitation • Jesus frees us from sin and puts us into fellowship with a loving God • Becoming a disciple may be costly • We are tempted to seek security in our own fortress • God's grace gives us strength to take risks to follow Jesus.

"What would you say to a man who wants to walk one hundred and forty miles to Canterbury?" A middle-aged man in a natty suit was the only other person in the waiting room, and he eyed me carefully when I posed the question at the train station of Farnham village. It was Friday morning, and an early train had just brought me from London to southern England. My walking stick leaned into a corner, a wide-rimmed hat was perched on the bench beside me, and I was rummaging through a rucksack for mudguards to fasten around the cuffs of my trousers.

"I would say, . . . I wish I could go with you," the man replied with a smile. "I've often thought of doing a long-distance walk. But I have my own business, and if I leave, there's nobody to run it."

How strange, I thought, that this man who wants to walk would live for years in a village along one of the best footpaths in the British Isles, and never make time for a sustained journey through the hills.

Although Farnham is not where the Pilgrims' Way starts, it is an excellent place to join the old road. The trackway actually begins at Winchester, twenty-eight miles southeast of Farnham. At Farnham, though, the Pilgrims' Way breaks free from busy roads and rises to the lovely ridges of the North Downs.

For countless centuries this market village has been a crossroads for traffic from all directions. From Farnham, a medieval traveler could go south to the sea, west toward Stonehenge, north into London, or east to the great cathedral at Canterbury. Every direction was full of possibility.

Even in medieval times, though, most residents of the village probably were like the businessman I met. They had compelling reasons to stay where they were. The immediate pull of apparent security, well-established routine, and comfortable reputation all conspire to keep people from starting a pilgrimage.

Compelling Reasons to Follow Jesus

Some people yearn to explore footpaths but stay home because of other commitments. Many others do the same when considering an invitation to follow Jesus. A long-distance trackway holds the promise of challenge, beauty, hard work, and a memorable destination. A long-term commitment to Christian discipleship holds the promise of forgiveness, healing, hard work, and a destination of great hope.

Christian discipleship also has a cost that any new follower must consider. We see a modern businessman who wants to hike and cannot leave his work for a week or two in the hills. So whatever possessed Peter and his partners in a fishing business to abandon their livelihood and follow Jesus?

The three had just spent a hardworking and unproductive night of fishing. In the morning Jesus met them on shore and asked to use a boat as a platform for speaking to the crowds. Then Jesus had an even more perplexing request. He instructed Peter to go out into the water again and put down the nets that they had just finished cleaning. Peter and his helpers obeyed, and soon their nets were groaning with fish:

> So they signaled their partners in the other boat to come and help them. And they came and filled both boats, so that they began to sink. But when Simon Peter saw it, he fell down at Jesus' knees, saying, "Go away from me, Lord, for I am a sinful man!" For he and all who were with him were amazed at the catch of fish that they had taken; and so also were James and John, sons of Zebedee, who were partners with Simon. Then Jesus said to Simon, "Do not be afraid; from now on you will be catching people." When they had brought their boats to shore, they left everything and followed him. (Luke 5:7-11)

We cannot know the inner navigation that pointed Peter, James, and John away from business-as-usual to a seemingly risky life on the road. Perhaps the fishermen already had heard about Jesus, or had listened to him speak on an earlier occasion. Jesus had preached or performed miracles at Nazareth, Capernaum, and other towns or cities in the region where the fishermen worked. Reports about the new teacher "began to reach every place in the region" (Luke 4:37).

A Longing for Freedom in Jesus' Day

Many Jews in first-century Palestine were looking for a great teacher, king, and deliverer to come. At the time of Jesus, Palestine was firmly under control of the Roman empire, and had been since 63 B.C. Before that, a series of other empires had dominated the region (Babylonia, Persia, and Greece). Many Jews longed for their nation to throw off foreign control, to be completely free to serve the God of their forebears.

Galilee, a northern region of Palestine where many Jews lived, was a hotbed of revolution against Roman rule. Sixty miles to the south, in the Jewish capital of Jerusalem, religious teachers were reading ancient prophecies in the Hebrew Scriptures about a Messiah (a deliverer anointed by God). Some said the time was near for his appearance.

It is clear from the Gospel accounts that some people who listened to Jesus thought he was the Messiah who would make the Jews free once again from foreign rule. Jesus announced that God's Spirit was upon him to "bring good news to the poor, . . . release to the captives, . . . sight to the blind," and freedom to the oppressed (Luke 4:18).

Something about Jesus breathed *freedom.* Perhaps it was his dedication to God, his courage in the face of opposition, and his sense of self-worth and mission. But more than mere political independence was on Jesus' agenda. He intended to liberate the inner lives of men and women from the greed, hatred, and lust for power that make oppressive empires possible.

Jesus was not merely addressing *symptoms* of evil, such as the presence of occupying Roman soldiers in the villages of Galilee. Instead, he sought to change the *source* problem, a human tendency to ignore God and use others for selfish purposes. Jesus began to address the question of how to relate to occupying soldiers by healing the servant of a centurion (Luke 7:1-10) and by asking God to forgive those who drove nails into his hands (Luke 23:34).

These localized responses to a vast empire demonstrated the power of God to change the human heart, and to break the cycles of selfishness and revenge that lead to violence and hatred between peoples. Such a show of love must have startled those who wielded oppressive power, allowing them to see the potential for a new kind of relationship between mortals.

A Hunger for Soul-Healing

I believe Peter and his fellow fishermen followed Jesus because they sensed in him a power of God that could set them free from patterns of life that destroy. When Jesus got into Peter's boat and taught the crowd, Peter had opportunity to hear the full message. Luke doesn't record what Jesus said, but we assume it was the same kind of teaching found elsewhere in the Gospels: God's extravagant forgiveness, God's great love for those who recognize their spiritual need, Jesus' frustration with people who smugly think that by their own power they are good enough for God.

It is paradoxical that men and women find freedom in giving complete allegiance to God. Modern Western societies place such value on independence and individualism that we might think relying on God would be a step backward. But a soul-virus infects the whole of humanity, a self-centeredness that is itself bondage. In every person there is a tendency to say, "I am of age now, and I don't need God. I can make my own decisions about right and wrong."

This is what eating from the tree represents in the story of Adam and Eve. That fruit "was to be desired to make one wise" (Genesis 3:6). They were following a drive toward self-serving independence. The Bible calls this "sin," a word that means "to miss the mark."

At some point in our lives, when we're trying to steer our own course through right and wrong, we realize we've made a mess of things. Perhaps we've been dishonest to friends, to ourselves, or to people we love in order to feed some financial, social, or sexual appetite. Perhaps we feel so inadequate or worthless inside that we know our outer appearance of confidence is a sham. Perhaps we've been victims of violence or abuse, or have inflicted the same on others. We may come to a point of self-loathing and despair. We may seem to be coping well with life, but have a hunger for soul-healing that cannot be put into words.

Peter must have been at such a point of crisis in his life. After Jesus filled the discouraged fishermen's nets with fish, Peter fell on his knees and cried, "Go away from me, Lord, for I am a sinful man!" Peter was afraid—perhaps afraid that someone so whole would make him feel more worthless. Would God punish him through this teacher who acted with divine power?

Jesus spoke words of reassurance: "Do not be afraid; from now on you will be catching people." Jesus accepted Peter. He also called Peter and other disciples to share in the task that was most important to Jesus himself: to put out the nets of God's love and forgiveness, to draw in other men and women who hungered to be whole, and to find meaning for their lives.

Leaving the Security of a Castle

The Pilgrims' Way passes immediately by the Farnham train station. But before starting east toward Canterbury, I took a half-mile detour through the village to the ruins of Farnham Castle. In its medieval heyday, the castle was a formidable palace, enclosed on all sides by massive stone walls and protected by a deep moat. Parts of the great walls survive, topped with turrets and window slits for archers. In the center of the whole complex is a deep well, to supply residents in the event of a siege.

The castle was entered by a drawbridge. A great doorway into the main courtyard featured a sliding gate with sharpened spikes that could be lowered quickly from above. Today we can still see a "murder hole" above the entryway through which excrement or boiling oil could be dropped, to repel attackers during a siege.

Everything about Farnham Castle smells of power, prestige, self-protection, and privilege—all defended by threats of force. That great fortress is a reminder of what men and women sometimes seek in our spiritual, social, and material lives.

We put others down to boost our own faltering egos. We are too proud to ask for forgiveness. We rejoice at the misfortune of

The 1619 Windsor Almshouses, below Farnham Castle

others. We are too selfish to be generous. We imagine that a larger savings account will make us happy. We forget that we are children of God. It may be dreary inside the castle of our isolation and self-sufficiency, but we crave security and will defend our spot on the hilltop.

At the bottom of the hill below Farnham Castle are the Windsor Almshouses, a row of little homes built in 1619 for needy people. A stone inscription on one of the gables announces that the structures were put there for the benefit of "Eight Poor Old Honest Impotent Persons." I felt more drawn to those humble houses than I did to the mighty castle. The almshouses seemed like a place where Jesus would have stopped to bring laughter and hope. Jesus started his best-known teaching, the Sermon on the Mount, with the words "Blessed are the poor in Spirit. . . . Blessed are the meek" (Matthew 5:3, 5).

> *A certain ruler asked him, "Good Teacher, what must I do to inherit eternal life?" Jesus said to him, "Why do you call me good? No one is good but God alone. You know the commandments: 'You shall not commit adultery; You shall not murder; You shall not steal; You shall not bear false witness; Honor your father and mother.' " He replied, "I have kept all these since my youth." When Jesus heard this, he said to him, "There is still one thing lacking. Sell all that you own and distribute the money to the poor, and you will have treasure in heaven; then come, follow me." But when he heard this, he became sad; for he was very rich.* (Luke 18:18-23)

In the Gospels, disciples of Jesus were people either already vulnerable or willing to become so. Peter the fisherman risked much when he left his home and job to follow Jesus. The wealthy ruler who inquired about inheriting eternal life was quite satisfied with the way he had followed the book of religious rules. But he was too attached to his possessions and his status to think of losing them. He might have lost some personal financial security. But he would have gained much more in belonging to a community of people whose lives were shaped by the values of Jesus.

Jesus said it is hard for those who have wealth to enter the kingdom of God (Luke 18:24). He did not mean that God has a particular dislike for people with material possessions or other sources of individual security. Rather, Jesus was simply observing that people who have such self-sufficiency often are unwilling to give it up for a greater gain in the kingdom of God.

A Hard Time to Become a Christian

Before leaving home to take a train to Farnham on the first day of my walk, I spoke at dawn with the first fellow pilgrim of my journey. Eileen Pells Coffman is a native Londoner and a resident at the London Mennonite Centre, where my family and I lived. "I'd love to have a new pair of legs," she laughed several times in the weeks before my journey. "Then I'd walk with you." But at age eighty-four, on the mend from a hip operation, she could not physically join me on the way.

On Friday morning Eileen waited for our conversation in housecoat and slippers, cane in hand. I asked what it meant for her to "leave everything and follow Jesus." Her mind scanned back over the decades to World War II in East London.

In 1940, near the beginning of the war, London was being heavily bombed. Thousands of people spent days or even weeks in underground shelters. My family and I usually went down overnight, to a shelter big enough for seven hundred people.

One Sunday evening a man from a local church came through the place inviting people to a worship service in one of the rooms. I took part, and worshiped with them every Sunday after that. One Sunday, when I had been asked to take a part in the service, I went out instead with a soldier friend. I didn't enjoy the evening and knew I had made a mistake. I knew God must come first in my life. From then on, I became serious about following Jesus.

At church I met John, who later became my husband. My friends knew he was a Christian, and called him the "sky pilot." I debated a lot of issues with him, including questions about the war. I thought we should fight back. But gradually I came to see that fighting was not Jesus' way of dealing with enemies.

I had picked a

Eileen Pells Coffman told about her early years as a Christian.

hard time to become a Christian and a peacemaker. My brother—who later died in the war—was in the merchant Navy. My sister was in an aircraft factory, making guns and bombs. I couldn't talk with my mother about what I believed because she came from an army family. When I told her I was going to join the church, she didn't say a word.

On the night I was baptized, I came home to find that the door to our house was locked. I spent that night with the neighbors. When mother found my baptism papers, she put them into the fireplace. But God gave me Christian friends. I quit my job selling umbrellas and sunshades at London Bridge, and worked with the Mennonite church, giving out clothes and food to people whose houses had been destroyed.

Eileen's decision to follow Jesus was costly. It (temporarily) alienated her from her family, and brought ridicule from some friends. Already before she was a Christian, the house she lived in was destroyed by a bomb. After becoming a disciple, she and her husband never owned a home. They always rented housing or lived in space provided by the church. They lived modestly, raised a family, and gave their lives to sharing the gospel.

Was Eileen richer or poorer for following Jesus? The fisherman Peter once worried about financial security in his own life. "Look," he said, "we have left our homes and followed you." Jesus replied that any one who has left "house or brothers or sisters or mother or father" for the sake of the gospel will get back "a hundredfold now *in this age* . . . and in the age to come eternal life" (Mark 10:28-30). Following Jesus is not a solo enterprise. We become part of a people who share materially and spiritually with each other.

A Staff in Slippery Places

Being a Christian and following Jesus is not something we do on our own strength and by our own force of will. When Jesus calls, he comes with the power of God to change us and sustain us for the pilgrimage. The Bible calls this the "grace" (*charis*) of God, a word that means help, goodwill, favor, or gift. God will give us what we need, spiritually and physically, and the "Spirit of Jesus" will go with us as surely as Jesus walked with Peter by the Sea of Galilee.

I was reminded of this gracious Presence after talking with Eileen. Members of the London Mennonite Centre household gathered for our usual time of morning prayer. That morning they used a prayer written by Benedictine monks centuries ago, for Christians about to set out on pilgrimage. The prayer starts with a reference to Abraham, father of the Jewish nation, whom God called to make a one-way pilgrimage to a promised land:

O God, who brought Abraham your servant out of Ur of the Chaldees, and preserved him unhurt throughout his journeyings, we beseech you to take Nelson under your protection. Be to him, O Lord, a support in setting out, a solace on the way, a shadow in the heat, a cover from the rain and cold, a chariot in weariness, a protection in danger, a staff in slippery places, and a harbor in shipwreck. Under your guidance may he happily reach the place whither he is going, and at length return to this home in safety. Through Jesus Christ our Lord, who lives and reigns with you and the Holy Spirit, world without end. Amen.

When the prayer ended, I donned my hat, hoisted the rucksack, picked up my walking stick, and headed out the door to the nearby Underground (subway) station.

When I got to central London by the subway, long trains slithered into Waterloo train station like silver snakes into a great urban cavern. The 8:25 train to Farnham arrived at my platform. Dozens of doors opened simultaneously, spilling out an avalanche of incoming commuters. I met them midstream, parting the flow of traffic as I headed the opposite direction.

The commuters were serious and well-dressed. They had briefcases in hand and were headed for the bowels of a great city, to banks and purchasing offices and government buildings. I realized how different I looked, and how different was my mission. The train that had trundled a thousand commuters into London now was virtually empty as it carried me in the opposite direction.

Prayer

Dear God, I yearn to know you fully and to follow Jesus in all of my life. Often I "miss the mark" of what you created me to be. Like the wealthy ruler, I am tempted to seek security in my own plans rather than in you. Let me be like Peter, ready to leave everything for the joy of being with Jesus. Amen.

For Reflection

1. What pressures or priorities keep people from following Jesus today?

2. What did Peter and other disciples lose when they became disciples? What did they gain?

3. In what ways do we seek security apart from God?

4. Can you think of ways that following Jesus might take us in a different direction from others around us?

Thirst for God

Friday, May 17: Farnham to Guildford (11 miles)

There is a hunger for meaning in our materialistic society • Our multireligious world has similarities to the environment in which the first Christians lived • Christians are tempted to ally themselves with wealth and power • Radical Christians through the centuries have sought to recover a simple lifestyle of obedience to Christ • We can learn from believers who have followed Jesus before us • Jesus will change us so we care about others caught in poverty or injustice.

Money-Rich and Spirit-Poor

The bulletin board of a small church near the train station in Farnham featured a magazine article on "The Empty Pew." It described a dramatic drop in church attendance among young people in England over the past decade. Despite this apparent loss of interest in the traditional church, the author said that young people are "the most impressionable and spiritually hungry section of the population." They are "anxious to find an alternative to materialism."

Not only young people, but all generations in the industrialized West seem bent on a search for meaning beyond career success, financial security, and recreation. If you survey titles in the psychology and religion section of almost any bookstore, you will find an astounding array of volumes on dreams, mysticism, astrology, crystal power, and new religions. In spite of our increased wealth and comfort, we are not satisfied. We are money-rich and spirit-poor.

A Simple Way of Obedience

In the first century, Christians were a small and politically suspect minority. They risked losing status or financial security if neighbors discovered their allegiance to Jesus. From the second century, we have evidence of charges against Christians. They were accused of being atheists because they didn't accept the Greek and Roman gods. Some people thought they were cannibals at their worship services because they spoke of "eating flesh and blood" (communion bread and wine; cf. John 6:52-58). They were suspected of being sexually immoral because they had secret "love-feasts" (Jude 12), with men and women taking part.

By the fourth century, however, Christianity was widespread across the Mediterranean world. Though Christians still were a minority, the emperor adopted Christianity and made it the official religion of the Roman empire. Within a hundred years, people were persecuted if they were *not* Christians.

For the next thousand years, the Christian church in Europe often was managed by people of wealth and political or military power. Jesus had called for his followers to rely on God rather than on material security. Not surprisingly, that call often got lost in the heady era of a powerful church.

As Christians allied themselves more and more with wealth and political power, some people sensed a decline in the spiritual vitality of the church. A few believers began to withdraw from comfortable society to live alone in deserts and mountains, seeking to recover a simple life of obedience to the example and teaching of Jesus.

Starting in the sixth century, Christian monastic communities sprang up across Europe. Monks and nuns in these communities typically made vows of poverty, chastity, and obedience to Christ. Most members—at least in the early years—lived disciplined lives of prayer, study, and simplicity. While some monastic communities physically separated themselves from contact with society, others engaged in mission and service to the world while rejecting the trappings of wealth and social power.

Remains of a Renewal Movement

Just outside Farnham, along the Pilgrims' Way, are the ruins of buildings from one such radical Christian community. This was the site of Waverly Abbey, established in 1128 by Cistercian monks from France. The Cistercian order had been founded by Bernard of Clairvaux, who sought to recover a gospel-based way of discipleship. Instead of relying on the money of others to support them (as did many monastic orders at that time), the Cistercians earned their own living through agriculture and trade. Members developed daily routines of worship, Bible reading,

The ruins of Waverly Abbey

prayer, and work. These disciplines are basic to the spiritual growth of Christians in any age.

Today only the ruins of Waverley Abbey stand like a monument at the edge of Farnham. Nothing of a living community survives. I approached the site on a dirt road, along the lovely River Wey. An old stone bridge still spans the water by the ruins, and a row of ducklings paddled away furiously as I approached. One large section of the ground floor of the Abbey still stands, with arched windows that long ago lost their glass. I stopped there to eat lunch in solitude and reflect on the tradition of monks who once inhabited the place.

Bernard of Clairvaux wrote that Christians typically pass through four stages or "degrees" of love:

- First, we love ourselves for our own sake; since we are unspiritual and of the flesh, we cannot have an interest in anything that does not relate to ourselves.
- When we begin to see that we cannot subsist by ourselves, we begin to seek God for our own sakes. This is the second degree of love. We love God, but only for our own interests.
- But if we begin to worship and come to God again and again by meditating, by reading, by prayer, and by obedience, little by little God becomes known to us through experience. We enter into a sweet familiarity with God. By tasting how sweet the Lord is, we pass into the third degree of love. Now we love God, not for our own sake, but for himself.
- Perhaps the fourth degree of love, in which we love ourselves only for the sake of God, may not be perfectly attained in this life. But when it does happen, we will experience the joy of the Lord and be forgetful of ourselves in a wonderful way. We are, for those moments, one mind and one spirit with God.

We seek God and follow Jesus because something is missing in our lives. This self-interest is not bad, because it turns us to God and gives us a desire for change. On a deep level, however, we are not able to move beyond self-interest without a relationship with God. The story of Jesus calling Peter to discipleship (see chapter 1) is an example of three "degrees of love" in response to God:

Peter first obeyed Jesus' instructions, "Put out into the deep water and let down your nets," because he was a fisherman who had wasted a night on the water with no catch (Luke 5:1-11). He had a personal interest in responding to Jesus (the "first degree" of love): a need to catch his daily quota.

When the nets filled with fish, then Peter knelt before Jesus in gratitude and fear. Beyond having failed at fishing the previous night, Peter realized his life was a failure. "Go away from me, Lord, for I am a sinful man!" he cried. Although verbally asking Jesus to leave, the act of kneeling was a moment of devotion rooted in fear of punishment and in recognition of his need for forgiveness (the "second degree" of love).

Jesus then said, "From now on you will be catching people." The call to discipleship did more than give Peter a clear conscience. Jesus called Peter to a way of life that pointed away from simple self-interest to living for God and others (the "third degree" of love).

The rest of the story of Peter in the Gospels and Acts tells of his struggle to move beyond self-love to an unshakable devotion to Jesus. Peter changed only gradually. When Jesus was arrested, Peter went through a terrible night of denying he ever knew him. But after Peter saw the empty tomb on Easter, and after he experienced the power of the Holy Spirit at Pentecost, he became a fearless messenger of hope to the world.

The words of Bernard of Clairvaux in the "fourth degree of love" match the experience of Peter in his mature witness for Christ. He experienced the joy of the Lord and forgot himself. The Gospel of John tells a story of Jesus, after his death and resurrection, testing the love of Peter:

> *Jesus said to Simon Peter, "Simon son of John, do you love me more than these?" He said to him, "Yes, Lord; you know that I love you." Jesus said to him, "Feed my lambs." A second time he said to him, "Simon son of John, do you love me?" He said to him, "Yes, Lord; you know that I love you." Jesus said to him, "Tend my sheep." He said to him the third time, "Simon son of John, do you love me?" Peter felt hurt because he said to him the third time, "Do you love me?" And he said to him, "Lord, you know everything; you know that I love you." Jesus said to him, "Feed my sheep. Very truly, I tell you, when you were younger, you used to fasten your own belt and to go wherever you wished. But when you grow old, you will stretch out your hands, and someone else will fasten a belt around you and take you where you do not wish to go." (He said this to indicate the kind of death by which he would glorify God.) After this he said to him, "Follow me." (John 21:15-19)*

Jesus wanted to know whether Peter's love for him was more than a sentimental commitment. Was Peter willing to take up the task of "feeding lambs" and "tending sheep"? Was he willing to get on with the day-to-day work of caring for those in spiritual and physical need? Was Peter willing to follow Jesus even if it meant facing death at the hands of those who would be threatened by the gospel? In these words, Jesus stripped discipleship of romance, laid out the costly path of obedience, and repeated words that Peter had heard when he first met Jesus: "Follow me."

Bernard of Clairvaux recognized that God wants those who love him to learn to love themselves (the "fourth degree" of love). Our initial encounter with God might bring disgust at the mess we've made of our lives. We will continue to be aware of our sin and failure, even after years of following Jesus. But by walking with Jesus in worship, prayer, and obedience, we also will come to know how deeply God loves us.

If God loved us so much that he sent Jesus to live and die for us, we have worth in God's eyes. With that knowledge, we can love ourselves as God loves us: as creatures of dignity and creativity. Secure in God's love and in acceptance of ourselves, we have an emotional and spiritual base to help bring hope and healing to the world around us.

The Wisdom of the Road

Not until I passed through Puttenham village, halfway to Guildford, did I finally get onto a section of the original Pilgrims' Way. On most of the walk to Canterbury, I could tell immediately when I reached a stretch of the old road. The Pilgrims' Way often is ten or twelve feet wide, worn down by the hoofs of countless horses and the feet of numberless travelers. Like a miles-long ancient scar—sometimes as deep as I am tall—the old road usually lies near the top of the ridge, on the south side.

The Pilgrims' Way almost never makes a sharp turn, and it typically passes close by the south side of churches along the way. The North Downs have a thick layer of chalkstone just below the surface. That provides better drainage for a footpath than would the valleys below. Gnarled yew trees that look as old as the hills stand guard at regular intervals along the roadside.

There is wisdom in the old road, practical considerations of route and terrain that generations of pilgrims found to be trustworthy. The same is true for believers today who immerse themselves in Scripture, learn from disciples in other centuries, and talk with other pilgrims along the way. Such people follow the wisdom of another old road.

Before Jesus' followers first were called "Christians," they were known as people of "The Way" (Acts 9:2; 11:26). We don't have to reinvent every aspect of Christian discipleship each generation. Although Jesus calls each man and woman afresh, we can learn from the path marked out by everyone from the apostle Paul to believing members of our own household.

The River Wey meanders through the countryside from where I started walking at Farnham. Eventually it cuts through the North Downs hills at Guildford—my destination for the first day of the journey. I approached town on the towpath of the river, where horses and mules once strained to pull canal boats into town.

That entrance to Guildford must be one of the loveliest to a town anywhere. I was enthralled by brightly painted canal boats that chugged by me as I walked. A boat named *Promise* slowly eased by, with a man and woman at the helm. "It's too cool for May!" the skipper called out in a friendly tone. I nodded; it had been an unusually chilly day for late spring. "I'm staying nice and warm," I answered, picking up my walking pace. "We're on our honeymoon," he volunteered, "and we'll stay nice and warm tonight!" I laughed at his comment and wished them well.

It occurred to me that *Promise* is a good name for a honeymoon boat. The decision to marry is not unlike a commitment to follow Jesus. Several times the New Testament compares the relationship between Jesus and the church to a marriage. Wedding vows and a commitment to follow Jesus both have lifelong implications. Just as marriage cannot depend upon a constant tide of romance to sustain it, Christian discipleship cannot rely upon spiritual euphoria or ecstatic experiences of God.

Marriage without any romance would be tedious, and discipleship without any emotional or spiritual hilltops would be drudgery. But in the end, it is commitment and decision that

The canal boat *Promise* at Guildford

sustain both marriage and discipleship, not romance or euphoria. When we are convinced that Jesus has called us to follow, we are able to take up difficult work for the kingdom and continue in discipleship even at times of doubt or suffering.

Friends of the Amos Trust

I trudged on weary legs up through Guildford, past old timbered houses and crooked storefronts. My rucksack stayed gladly at a bed-and-breakfast house while I walked on further to meet a circle of generous Christians who had invited me to dinner. A meal was spread out at the vicarage of St. John's Church, hosted by the minister, Stephen Sizer. Stephen and three others who joined us are all involved in a justice project called the Amos Trust, based in Guildford.

The Amos Trust is a music and teaching project that educates people in wealthy nations about needs of the developing world. Years ago when singer Garth Hewitt was visiting Haiti, someone there said, "You will never forget what you've seen here, and you must never be silent about it or forget those who have no voice."

Out of that experience, Hewitt founded the Amos Trust, which helps finance a variety of projects around the world. These include a children's home in South Africa, schoolbooks for Palestinian children, housing in Nicaragua, and a well in Uganda.

In a book called *Pilgrims and Peacemakers*, Garth Hewitt writes,

> We discover that the road to personal peace and satisfaction does not lie in putting ourselves first; it doesn't lie in ignoring the conflicts and the pain in our world; it doesn't lie in keeping quiet about issues of justice. It is those who hunger and thirst for justice who will find satisfaction; it is those who lose their life who will gain it, those who give their lives for others and who refuse to allow bigotry, prejudice, and selfishness to dominate. Following Jesus is not just a geographical exercise; it is a way of life. It is an attitude of mind and heart, it is taking up a cross, it is being a servant.

Responding to Human Need

At dinner, Stephen Sizer introduced me to Beki Bateson, Projects Coordinator for the Amos Trust. Also joining the meal were John Alleyne (an adviser on immigration and refugee issues for the Church of England) and Margaret Blake (a Church of England curate and support worker for people on probation).

Beki explained that the name "Amos Trust" was inspired by the Old Testament prophet of that name. Amos announced that God rejected the pious religious observances of people who didn't care about the well-being of others:

I hate, I despise your festivals,
and I take no delight in your solemn assemblies.
Even though you offer me your burnt offerings
and grain offerings,
I will not accept them;
and the offerings of well-being of your fatted animals
I will not look upon.
Take away from me the noise of your songs;
I will not listen to the melody of your harps.
But let justice roll down like waters,
and righteousness like an everflowing stream.
(Amos 5:21-24)

Jesus firmly rooted his teaching and ministry in the words and example of Hebrew prophets such as Isaiah and Amos. These prophets had worked and taught hundreds of years before Jesus. They often made a close link between faith in God and care for those in physical need.

"In Guildford, it's easy to ignore suffering because you don't have to see poverty," Stephen declared. He told about making a trip to Israel and meeting Palestinian people who had been pushed off their land. "I either had to ignore the suffering of the Palestinians and say they're just terrorists, or I had to get involved and do something. I realized Palestinians are real people; they have children like mine."

During the tense days of the Cold War, Stephen met Christians in the Soviet Union. "I had to change my attitude about nuking people who were part of the body of Christ," he said. In both cases, he explored the issues and began to speak with other Christians in Britain about ways to respond. "When we really face people who are suffering," Beki noted, "we want to respond. Not everyone can go to another country. So our job at the Amos Trust is to raise awareness. We brought Palestinians to Britain and have partners in various parts of the world."

John Alleyne joined the conversation, emphasizing that many issues of justice and need are close to home even in developed countries. "I spent part of today with a refugee mother and her three children whom the government was threatening to deport. Not long ago I helped organize bail for twenty Kurdish refugees who were being kept in prison."

Good News About Something That Really Works

Conversation shifted to a discussion of how we share our faith with others. "A lot of evangelism is verbal and manipulative," Margaret Blake said. "If our walk with Jesus changes our lives and makes a difference in the world around us, others will notice, and we naturally will want to talk about our faith."

At this point Stephen Sizer sprang to his feet, went to a back room, and returned with an odd-looking new vacuum cleaner. We all laughed, but he energetically explained that this innovative piece of equipment is the most efficient vacuum cleaner he's ever used. It features a transparent cylinder with a rotating unit that creates a vacuum. The force of the vacuum remains constantly strong, even when the machine is almost full of dirt.

"The standard vacuum cleaner loses three-fourths of its power by the time the bag is full," he claimed with conviction. "The point is, we get excited about something that works. If we're going to get involved in evangelism, we must have a faith that works and that people can see."

Stephen pulled out a quote by Eberhard Arnold which emphasizes that showing the love of Christ is something we do in small local ways, not just in big projects overseas:

> Unless we prove our readiness to die for God's kingdom in the trivialities of daily life, we shall not be able to muster up the courage in the critical hour of history.

"For me, the 'trivialities' might be treating a tramp in Guildford as if he were Christ," Stephen said.

"That cannot just be a one-time act," added Beki, "but we continue to treat the tramp like Christ. If our vision of the gospel is all in the future, it doesn't demand much of us today. We must be Jesus today."

Margaret led us in prayer before the group scattered, remembering particularly "those for whom the kingdom is yet to come: the poor, the homeless, the Palestinians, the people of East Timor, and . . ." The list went on

Reverend Stephen Sizer, minister at St. John's Church in Guildford

for a while, as she called for God's mercy upon suffering people around the world.

Prayer

Dear God, thank you that you care for me even when I hurt or when I am unlovely. I need to know that you accept me so I can accept myself. Give me your joy and peace, so I have something to give to those around me. Open my eyes to see the needs of others near and far, and teach me to respond with the love of Jesus. Amen.

For Reflection

1. Do you recognize among friends or within yourself a hunger for meaning beyond material or social success? How do people seek to satisfy such hunger?

2. Can you identify any changing "degrees of love" in your own response to God? Did some personal need bring you to seek God?

3. Are there any believers you have known or heard about that inspire you to follow Jesus? Why do you find them helpful or attractive?

4. What justice issues (of wealth, power, social position, or prejudice) do you think Christians today need to take seriously?

3

Choose the Better Part

Saturday, May 18: Guildford to Dorking (12 miles)
Fellow pilgrims: Ellen, Laura, and Andrea Kraybill

Sunday, May 19: Dorking to Merstham (9 miles)
Fellow pilgrim: Jane Schofield

*Doing many tasks for God cannot be a substitute for a living
relationship with Jesus • We need to make time to sit at Jesus' feet
to learn how discipleship is done • Forgiving enemies is one
of the hardest lessons to learn • We are tempted to base
our security on material things rather than on God •
We need a faith community around us to enable us
to live out the teachings of Jesus.*

Overlooking Vanity Fair

Sleep came easily after miles of walking and a hot bath. I awoke the next morning with sore muscles but a glad heart. It was Saturday morning. My wife, Ellen, and our daughters, Laura (13) and Andrea (8), had planned to take a train from London to Guildford, to join me for a day on the road.

Low, dark clouds frowned upon me as I made my way across town after a hearty feed at the bed-and-breakfast. Three enthusiastic walkers hugged me on the railway platform. Together we bought supplies for the day: bread, lunch meat, boxes of juice, peanuts, chocolate, and fruit.

We walked up the steep high street of Guildford (which Charles Dickens called "the loveliest in the entire kingdom") to a sports shop. Andrea now was old enough to carry a rucksack, and we needed to buy her a good one. It was nearly eleven o'clock by the time we headed out of town, down the towpath by the canal, across a footbridge, and up into the hills.

Below us, a short distance across the valley, we could see the hamlet of Shalford Common. In the seventeenth century, there was a year-round market and fair in this village. John Bunyan, author of *The Pilgrim's Progress,* knew this village, and some scholars think he may have used its marketplace as an inspiration for his description of Vanity Fair. The main character of Bunyan's book is Christian, who with a fellow pilgrim must pass through Vanity Fair on his way to the Celestial City.

[At Vanity Fair] are all such merchandise sold, as houses, lands, trades, places, honours, preferments, titles, countries, kingdoms, lusts, pleasures, and delights of all sorts, as whores, bawds, wives, husbands, children, masters, servants, lives, blood, bodies, souls, silver, gold, pearls, precious stones, and what not. . . .

The Prince of Princes himself, when here, went through this Town to his own country, and that upon a fair-day too. Yea, and as I think it was Beelzebub, the chief lord of this Fair, that invited him to buy of his vanities; yea, and would have made him lord of the Fair, would he but have done him [Beelzebub] reverence as he went through the town. Yea, because he was such a person of honour, Beelzebub led him from street to street, and showed him all the kingdoms of the world in a little time, that he might if possible allure that Blessed One, to cheapen and buy some of his vanities.

[People of the town take notice as Christian and his fel-

Laura (13), Andrea (8), and Ellen on the lovely high street of Guildford

low pilgrim walk through.] First, the pilgrims were clothed with such kind of raiment as was diverse from the raiment of any that traded in that Fair. The people therefore of the Fair made a great gazing upon them: Some said they were fools, some they were bedlams, and some "They are out-landish-men." [But] . . . that which did not a little amuse the merchandisers was that these pilgrims set very light by all their wares, they cared not so much as to look upon them.

Bunyan's comment about the Prince of Princes having been invited by Beelzebub (Satan) to "buy of his vanities" in this town refers to the temptation of Jesus in the wilderness (Luke 4:1-13). Satan offered Jesus distractions, detours, and shortcuts to success:

Turn stones into bread (satisfy your own physical appetite, and perhaps gain a following by feeding others). Seize political power (and perhaps throw out the Roman army by insurrection). Jump off the pinnacle of the temple and let God miraculously save you (and perhaps win the praise and awe of spectators).

Jesus rejected all three options. Instead, he chose the difficult way of obedience, joy, and suffering that God placed before him.

Making Time to Sit at Jesus' Feet

Our daughters were in a lyrical mood. Even on a cloudy day, the beauty of the woods inspired Laura to begin a poem: "Lacy flowers on either side, mark the path where I abide. . . ." Andrea, looking like a puppy in her big new boots, observed that "free music from the birds makes walking even better."

We climbed a long slope to the top of a ridge where a little church known as St. Martha's on the Hill has stood for eight hundred years. Although rebuilt a century ago, the church still has a medieval atmosphere about it. The hill upon which it stands apparently once was a center of pagan worship. Tradition

The eight-hundred year-old church of St. Martha's on the Hill

says Christians were martyred here. No other church building in England is named for Martha, the woman who once hosted Jesus for a meal in her own home and grew impatient at needing to do all the dinner preparation herself.

> Now as they went on their way, he entered a certain village,
> where a woman named Martha welcomed him into her home.
> She had a sister named Mary, who sat at the Lord's feet and
> listened to what he was saying. But Martha was distracted by
> her many tasks; so she came to him and asked, "Lord, do you
> not care that my sister has left me to do all the work by my-
> self? Tell her then to help me." But the Lord answered her,
> "Martha, Martha, you are worried and distracted by many
> things; there is need of only one thing. Mary has chosen the
> better part, which will not be taken away from her." (Luke
> 10:38-42)

Martha "was distracted by her many tasks" while her sister,
Mary, sat at Jesus' feet and listened to him. In several ways, Jesus
was breaking Jewish religious customs of his day: He was alone
with women who were not his relatives. He allowed a woman to
serve him. And he was teaching a woman in her home.

Jesus' actions demonstrated his desire for the good news of
the kingdom to break down society's stereotypical roles for men
and women. He was calling both women and men to prepare for
significant roles in the kingdom of God.

Martha, busy *doing* for Jesus, became frustrated with a sister
who sat listening while another person worked. Jesus addressed
Martha in her irritation, and the repetition of Martha's name
suggests that he spoke gently: "Martha, Martha, you are worried
and distracted by many things; there is need of only one thing.
Mary has chosen the better part, which will not be taken away
from her."

Elsewhere in his teaching, Jesus calls his followers to be servants. Hence, he was not rebuking Martha for preparing a meal.
His point was about priorities: unless we find time to sit at Jesus'
feet and be in fellowship with him, our acts of service will not
bring enduring life to ourselves or others.

Mary was strengthening her relationship with Jesus, learning from him, and building a base of understanding and inner character that could not be taken away. She would always know that *Jesus honored women in a society that often didn't, and that he cared specifically about her. Mary would carry a sense of mission imparted by a teacher who explained what discipleship meant, and who applied kingdom values to her life and gifts.

A Lesson from the Bell-Ringer

We had the good fortune of finding St. Martha's church unlocked when we stepped up to the arched doorway. Inside the

dark interior, the caretaker, Mr. Turner, met us. Bundled in scarf and coat against the chill of a damp day, he took us on a tour of the place.

A modern conversation piece of the ancient building is a prayer cushion belonging to Sir George Edwards, a member of the congregation who designed the Concorde supersonic passenger jet. The cushion features a likeness of the aircraft, a reminder of how human society has changed since Christians put up that meeting place almost a millennium ago.

Andrea, Laura, and church caretaker Mr. Turner with the Concorde supersonic jet prayer cushion

Mr. Turner asked Andrea if she would like to ring the church bell. "We don't allow boys to ring it," he said seriously, "because the rope has been broken twice. Boys leap onto the rope like Tarzan, and then there's a dreadful clattering of broken parts in the belfry."

Mr. Turner placed his large hand on top of Andrea's on the bell rope, and gently showed her how to set up a rhythm that sounded the bell high above. As soon as she mastered the beat, he let go and watched with a broad smile as she carried on with the ringing.

Just as Martha and Mary learned discipleship from Jesus, Andrea learned bell-ringing from the master. Discipleship, I thought, works that way. We need to see how it's done, and let the hand of a gentle master guide us to the daily rhythms of obedience and witnessing.

Forgiving the Enemy

It was starting to rain when we emerged from the chapel. I realized I had a stiff back, sore arms, and aching legs. My feet felt like they were in a vice, hurting with every step. We paused for a quick meal before pressing on. The girls cheered us up with silly book-title jokes (such as *Fell off a Cliff*, by Eileen Dover).

Birds sounded exuberant in the light rain as we got into the forest again, and a soft carpet of bluebells covered the ground on either side. Gorse bushes with yellow flowers were everywhere, and Andrea tried to steal up on lambs when we crossed a meadow. To our right, through fog and light rain, we could see a wide valley stretched out below with hedgerows marking the lines where green and brown fields met each other.

At a number of places that day we came across pillboxes, World War II bunkers nestled into upper slopes of the North Downs. Little fortresses twenty feet across, they have thick cement walls with a brick outer layer, and a hefty slab of concrete

Laura and Andrea inspecting a World War II pillbox fortress

for a roof. They were built to defend London against a feared invasion from the continent in the 1940s. Like sinister eyes, dark slits showed on their fronts, from which guns could be fired.

Andrea and Laura peered cautiously into a pillbox window after Ellen and I explained their purpose. The rain had stopped, and it was a good setting for our daily Scripture and prayer. Our Old Testament passage was Psalm 130, which reads,

> *If you, O Lord, should mark iniquities,*
>   *Lord, who could stand?*
> *But there is forgiveness with you,*
>   *so that you may be revered.*
> *I wait for the Lord, my soul waits,*
>   *and in his word I hope;*
> *my soul waits for the Lord*
>   *more than those who watch for the morning,*
>   *more than those who watch for the morning.*

O Israel, hope in the Lord!
For with the Lord there is steadfast love,
  and with him is great power to redeem.
It is he who will redeem Israel from all its iniquities.

(Psalm 130:3-8)

We pondered the forgiveness and mercy of God, and the human instinct to hurt or even kill when we feel threatened. We talked about Hitler and the crimes his government committed in Europe, particularly against the Jews. Even a child could recognize that something evil had been in the air half a century ago. We could understand why people of Britain wanted to defend themselves.

"People in a bunker like this were trying to protect themselves and get other people," Laura said pensively.

It made sense, but was a threat of committing further violence the way of Jesus?

> The author of Psalm 130 recognized that all humans have evil in our hearts: "If you, O Lord, should mark iniquities, Lord, who could stand?" No one in our family has ever shot a gun at another person or helped round up people for execution. But we all recognized a selfish streak within, a temptation to cut others with words or otherwise to retaliate at school, at work, or at home. Warfare is an expression of the same instinct, but with lethal tools of destruction and on a tribal or international level.

The psalmist brought awareness of inner sin to God. Jesus taught his disciples to do the same with this phrase from the Lord's Prayer: "Forgive us our sins, for we ourselves forgive everyone indebted to us" (Luke 11:4; cf. Matthew 6:12, NCV). Our attitude toward people who sin against us is closely related to God's forgiveness of our sin. We must know the love and power of God in order to forgive others—and we must forgive others in order to know the love and power of God. We cannot have one without the other.

A Story of Forgiveness

The topic of forgiving enemies reminded our family about a survivor of one of Hitler's concentration camps, in a story we had read some years earlier:

Corrie ten Boom's family hid Jews in Holland during World War II. Her [entire] family [including Corrie herself] was sent to concentration camps. Only Corrie survived. After the war, Corrie was in Germany speaking on forgiveness. In one church, a man caught her eye. As he spoke with her, she remembered seeing him in a Nazi uniform. He had been a guard at Ravensbruck, the camp where she and her sister were imprisoned.

Never since the end of the war had Corrie before been faced with one of her oppressors. He complimented her [for her] sermon and tried to shake her hand, but she could not. He told her that he had been a guard at Ravensbruck and had since become a Christian.

"I know that God has forgiven me for the cruel things I did there, but I would like to hear it from your lips. Fräulein, will you forgive me?" He tried again to shake her hand. But Corrie could not forgive, even though she knew what Jesus taught.

Feeling no forgiveness, she woodenly, mechanically thrust her hand into his outstretched one. As she did, an incredible thing happened. A current started in her shoulder, raced down her arm, and sprang into their joined hands. Its healing warmth flooded her entire being.

"I forgive you, Brother," she said through her tears, "with my whole heart." For a long moment, the former guard and former prisoner grasped each other's hands.

Corrie ten Boom closes this account by writing: "I had never known God's love so intensely as I did then."[1]

It seemed certain to us that such forgiveness would be impossible without the love of God. Unless we spend time sitting at Jesus' feet, listening to his teaching, and experiencing the same Spirit that empowered him, we will not know how to forgive.

Extra Miles on Weary Legs

We had a street address for the vicarage of an Anglican church in North Holmwood. The minister and his wife had kindly offered to give us lodging. We thought the address was within the town of Dorking, just off the Pilgrims' Way. When we entered the town on weary legs, we were surprised to learn that North Holmwood was another town several miles south of Dorking.

I was certain our hosts would be happy to pick us up by car, but I held my resolve to walk every inch of the journey. The family was of one mind: if I walked the rest of the way, so would they! We ate a quick pizza in Dorking, then trudged two long miles up over the hills along a busy road to our destination. A member of the congregation was watching for us as dusk approached, and showed us the way to the vicarage on the edge of the village green.

Our hosts were Warren and Erica Frederick—he an Anglican minister and she a United Reformed Church minister. Although I first met Warren in England, he was raised in Pennsylvania in my own denomination, and we had plenty to talk about. Warren has lived his adult life in England, and Erica is British. Both were out on church business when the neighbor let us into the house. We found our way to the bedrooms and gratefully prepared for the night.

Worship at North Holmwood

On Sunday morning I was to preach at Warren's church. I got up before the rest of the family to pray and organize my thoughts. At eight o'clock the sound of church bells filtered into the bedroom, and I realized that Warren already was leading the early service. Our family had a leisurely breakfast, then made our way across the village green for the late service.

I was ushered into the vestry, where a great flurry of gowns, candles, Bibles, and religious vessels filled the room. Warren wore a white robe, and the others wore black. I was in walking clothes, with boots and trouser mudguards, carrying my walking stick and hat. Musicians and worship leaders shook my hand warmly, including the animated old organist, Chris Ward.

Chris has gray hair and laughing eyes, despite his long battle with hydrocephaly as a child and multiple sclerosis as an adult. He has "fits" and told me, almost jovially, that he soon was going to the hospital for major brain surgery.

"I've already been replumbed, rewired, and had a sump station put in," he laughed. Then, more serious, he added, "My condition makes me see double, and sometimes I play the organ almost blind."

I pondered the faith and optimism of a man for whom life is so precarious.

Bellows and pipes for the organ spilled over into the vestry, and loud music filled the space when Chris began to play. Warren gathered the choir and worship leaders together for prayer. Then we all went out a side door, along the outside of the building, and into the rear of the sanctuary.

The congregation of eighty worshipers rose to their feet, the organ pushed toward full volume, and the choir began to sing as in procession we went down the aisle. Candle-bearers and a cross led the way; Warren and I followed. I sat down at the wrong place (on the front seat of the choir section!) and politely got moved.

There followed prayer, Gospel reading, communion, and liturgy. Then it was time for me to preach. The raised podium

Chris Ward, organist at the Anglican Church in North Holmwood

looked too formal for my attire and my theology, so I stood between the first pews, in the center aisle. After a few introductory
comments, I began with the story of an early martyr among my
Anabaptist forebears:

> In 1573 a young mother named Maeyken van Deventer was
> put to death for her Anabaptist convictions at Rotterdam in
> Holland. Shortly before she died, she wrote a letter of testa-
> ment for her children, and it is striking for its attitude to-
> ward material things:[2]
>
> "Albert, Johan, Egbert, Truyken, my dear children. The
> Lord bless you, as Isaac blessed his son Jacob. . . . I must
> leave you young. . . . I cannot leave you gold or silver, nor
> can I give you treasures of this world. . . . Children, love

your neighbor heartily, and with a liberal heart. Let the light of the Gospel shine in you. Deal your bread to the hungry, clothe the naked, and do not suffer anything to remain with you double, since there are enough that lack. And whatsoever the Lord grants you, that possess with thankfulness, not only for yourselves, but also for your neighbor, and seek not your own profit, but that of your neighbor. In short, my children, let your life be conformed to the Gospel of Christ."

Here was a woman who had a clear sense that following Jesus meant a fundamental change in priorities. The cost of discipleship for her was extraordinarily high: separation from family, loss of all material goods, and the death of a martyr. Notice, though, how she counsels her children to handle material goods: possess your goods with thankfulness to God, . . . but also feed the hungry, don't keep more than you need when others are in want, and seek the well-being of others around you. "In short, . . . let your life be conformed to the Gospel of Christ."

After the sixteenth century with its persecution, some Mennonites in Europe went on to become wealthy and secure in society. A leading Mennonite minister in the seventeenth century was praised by poets and could afford to have his portrait painted by Rembrandt. An elder of the church to which that minister belonged reflected on the change that overtook Mennonites when they became more comfortable: "When our houses were of wood, our hearts were of gold, but when our houses became golden, our hearts became wooden."

It's easy to be critical of others and their possessions, and not realize the hold materialism has on our own lives. A story about a young man being interviewed for membership in the Communist party illustrates the difference between theory and personal practice:

A party official asked the young candidate what he would do if he had £100,000. "That's easy," was the response, "I'd give £50,000 to the party."

"What would you do if you have two houses?" Without hesitation the answer came, "I'd give one to the party and live in the other."

"And what if you had two pairs of trousers?" There was a long silence.

"Why the hesitation?" asked the interviewer. "Because I *have* two pairs of trousers," replied the young man.

How tightly do we hold onto our goods? How does our practice measure up to the theory of the Gospels? Jesus calls us to a high standard of discipleship, and he often speaks of obedience in financial terms. Jesus has startling words about how we should manage our budgets: "I tell you, do not worry about your life, what you will eat, or about your body, what you will wear. . . . Sell your possessions and give alms. . . . For where your treasure is, there your heart will be also" (Luke 12:22, 33-34).

How do you suppose these words about not worrying fell on the ears of the peasants and day workers and marginalized people who made up the bulk of the crowds following Jesus? Sociologists, attempting to reconstruct the society in which Jesus spoke, estimate that the population of Palestine was at least 90 percent peasant. These were people with little economic or social power, who were largely at the mercy of a small number of landholders and lenders.

Some peasants listening to Jesus may have had access to land, but many would have carried a hefty weight of debt. Even the most insignificant landholder had to give up nearly 40 percent of his harvest simply to pay taxes or to make the required tithes to the Jewish temple. The Romans got their share of the tax pie, with aggressive tax collectors such as Zacchaeus making certain everybody paid. In Jesus' parables, the themes of debt and un-employment appear several times, suggesting these may have been familiar problems to his listeners.

In the Sermon on the Mount (Matthew 5—7) Jesus tells his followers, "Do not store up for yourselves treasures on earth," and warns "you cannot serve God and money" (6:19, 24). Jesus says, "Do not be anxious about tomorrow; tomorrow will look after itself" (6:34, REB). When I hear people dismiss the teachings of Jesus as noble but impractical, usually they cite either the call for us to love our enemies or the call for us not to worry about money. It sounds like a sentimental idea that God will take care of me just like he cares for the lilies. Maybe that worked back in a peasant, agrarian, preindustrial society in which people just ate off the fat of the land; but you cannot live that way in London or Dorking!

In our passage (Luke 12:31), Jesus says we should not worry about food and clothing, because God our Father knows we need these things. "But strive for [God's] kingdom, and these things will be given to you as well." In practical terms, how does this happen?

The Gospel of Mark (10:17-31) records the incident of a wealthy man who wanted to inherit eternal life. The man claimed to have lived a godly, exemplary life. Mark says Jesus "looked at him and loved him," then said, "One thing you lack: Go sell everything you have and give to the poor." The man was unwilling to follow Jesus' counsel, and left with a heavy heart.

Almost as an aside, Jesus remarks to his disciples, "How hard it will be for those who have wealth to enter the kingdom of God! . . . It is easier for a camel to go through the eye of a needle than for someone who is rich to enter the kingdom of God" (10:23, 25).

At that point, Peter spoke up, perhaps a bit worried: "[Jesus,] we have left everything to follow you!" And then Jesus goes on to address the worry Peter must have felt about giving up his security: "Truly I tell you, there is no one who has left home, brothers or sisters, mother, father or children, or land, for my sake and for the gospel, who will not receive in this age a hundred times as much, . . . and in the age to come eternal life" (10:28-30, REB).

A hundred times as much in this present age! From where does such wealth come for people who give up their possessions? Do you remember that time in the Gospels when someone mentioned Jesus' family? Jesus replied "My mother and my brothers are those who hear the word of God and act upon it," put it into practice (Luke 8:21, REB). In other words, if following Jesus means you must leave a family which does not understand your call, then you will find a new family among those who practice the kingdom of God. You will find a place to belong.

This belonging is more than just a social connection. For Jesus, the new faith community forming around his teaching was his place of belonging and financial security. Do you know how Jesus and the disciples financed their preaching tours around Palestine? Luke reports that some women among the disciples "provided for them out of their own resources" (Luke 8:1-3, REB). One of these disciples was Joanna, wife of Chuza, the manager of Herod's household. Imagine, the wife of Herod's steward funding the gospel!

Some of Jesus' followers were wealthy, and they made their money available for the work of the kingdom. Jesus' way of not worrying about money was to belong to a community where members actually shared resources.

The Amish, from the area where I was raised in Pennsylvania, have a sense of communal security. If a barn burns down, the entire neighborhood comes together, pools financial resources, and hammers together a new barn. Lest you think that's a great idea that might work only in rural Pennsylvania, consider the congregation here in England with whom our family spent Easter weekend one year.

A couple in that church, with limited financial resources, felt called by God to go overseas on a yearlong mission assignment. Others in the church said, "We'll pay your mortgage while you're gone." This is a congregation with many unemployed members, but there is a feeling of plenty in the church because members genuinely share.

A deep level of spiritual, emotional, and financial sharing is not possible if we think of our commitment to the kingdom of God as something pleasant which we occasionally do on the weekends. Jesus says, Seek *first* God's kingdom, and all this will be yours. When a group of people begin to think radically, and take Jesus' teaching and example seriously, something of the kingdom of heaven breaks into the world in surprising ways. We become light, salt, and leaven, a city set on a hill—providing an example and an invitation to a society in which people are run to exhaustion trying to find a secure place to belong (Matthew 5:13-16; 6:33; 13:33).

A Reordering of Priorities

With a few more comments, I finished my sermon. When the service was over, we went to the home of two members for a meal. Ellen and our daughters took a train back to London, while Jane Schofield—a member of the congregation where we had worshiped—joined me for the first stretch of walking that afternoon.

Jane's dog Rusty pulled hard on his collar as we walked up through Dorking, where a sudden rainstorm sent us running to a bus shelter for cover. When the rain stopped, we continued north of Dorking through a vast vineyard until our path joined the Pilgrims' Way. Seventeen stepping stones gave us dry passage on foot across the shallow River Mole. From there, the path climbed steeply up to scenic views on Box Hill.

A wife, mother, and former commodities broker, Jane talked about the way a health crisis changed her priorities:

Jane Schofield and her dog, Rusty

Five years ago I had a burst blood vessel in the brain, and
was rushed off to the hospital very ill. People thought I was
dying, and that experience changed my priorities. More
than ever before, I wanted to be with my children and family again. I also found out who my friends were. Some people
sent expensive bouquets of flowers, but it was people who

were there to hold the basin for me who were real friends.

I used to worry about death in terms of what would happen to me. Now I only think about what it would mean for my family. I do everything for God, and have a sense that it all has meaning—even the menial, such as cleaning up after a sick child in the nursery at church.

Wind and Rain

In midafternoon, Jane left the trail to go down into Reigate for a train back to Dorking. Again I was alone on the pathway. As the afternoon progressed, the weather became more and more tumultuous. From the top of a hill above Reigate, I watched rain pour down from dark clouds above the valley like windswept curtains hanging from a wash line. Trees bowed under the strain of wind, rain smacked into my cheeks, and I was glad for the chin strap on my hat. I wrapped a rain jacket tightly around my shoulders as the full force of a storm bore down.

In pouring rain, I emerged from the woods at Gatton. There a large fox slipped through the tall grass, crossed the path in front of me, and disappeared into the forest.

In late afternoon, the rain stopped, and a brilliant rainbow appeared ahead. One side of the arc reached down into a field of florescent yellow rape oil plant—as close as nature comes to planting a pot of gold at the end of a rainbow!

As I approached my night stop at the village of Merstham, I realized how strong the afternoon wind had been. A large white cricket backstop at the edge of a playing field had blown over across my path, completely obstructing the way and partly destroying the structure.

It was nearly 7:30 when I arrived at my hotel near the Merstham train station. A cook preparing my dinner suggested that I wait in the bar, where patrons in various states of sobriety engaged me in conversation. One talkative chap pointed across the room to a man who was "the former undisputed middle-weight boxing champion of the world." I did my best to look impressed, and was glad when the cook summoned me to a table.

Back in my room after dinner, I went through what had become my usual evening routine: wash boots, clean mud off mudguards, take a hot shower, write in my diary, and thank God for a place to sleep.

Prayer

Dear God, I find it hard to love those who hurt me—even in the day-to-day relationships of ordinary life. I find it difficult not to worry about money, not to want greater security in material things. If I am going to live out the dangerous love of Jesus, I need a daily relationship with you. Give me a deep awareness of your presence. Let me make time to sit at Jesus' feet, and plant me in the middle of a faith community where I can share with other disciples the joy and vulnerability of this way of life. Amen.

For Reflection

1. In what way did Mary find the "better part" of serving Jesus by sitting at his feet? Do you feel a tension in your life between learning from Jesus and carrying out your daily work responsibilities?

2. Whom do you find difficult to forgive? Why would God want someone like Corrie ten Boom to forgive a man who so grievously harmed her?

3. Why do material things affect our relationship with God? How should Christians plan for their financial future?

4. What examples have you seen of followers of Jesus supporting each other in living out the difficult sayings of Jesus?

Seventeen stepping-stones gave us dry passage across the River Mole.

4

Take Courage in Prayer

Monday, May 20: Merstham to Oxted (9 miles)
Fellow pilgrims: Howard and Sue Moss

*We need to learn how to pray • We pray to a God who has shown
himself to us as Father, Son, and Holy Spirit • Jesus emptied
himself of divine status to become human • We empty ourselves
of pretense and power to become effective for God • Through prayer,
God is changing us to be like Jesus • Prayer is as much listening
as it is speaking • Our inner spiritual life must issue in real
involvement in needs of the world.*

A Pilgrim's Walking Gear

"You look like something out of a time machine!" laughed
Howard Moss as he and his wife, Sue, met me on a footbridge
crossing the tracks at the Merstham railroad station. I had to
admit I was something of a spectacle with my broad-rimmed hat,
vest with sixteen(!) pockets, matching trousers, mudguards, sturdy boots, rucksack, and walking stick.

Not long after I arrived in England five years earlier, Howard
had explained to me what the British mean by "taking the Mickey out of" someone. It means using humor or even ridicule to
bring a pretentious person down to size. It would not be accurate
to say Howard ridiculed me in our years of friendship, but we
often laughed together and took the Mickey out of each other.

I examine a chunk of the chalkstone that lies just below the surface
along much of the Pilgrims' Way.

The hat I wore for the Pilgrims' Way invited merriment—even if I quickly came to treasure it for protection from the elements. A label inside reads, "This is the Tilley Hat. It is the best outdoor hat in the world. It floats, ties on, repels rain and mildew, won't shrink, and will be replaced free if it wears out. (Yes, put it in your will.) Ten-ounce, USA-treated cotton duck, solid British brass hardware, sewn with Canadian persnicketiness."

Inside the crown of the hat is a little pocket that holds "Brag Tags" with anecdotes about the Tilley Hat for the owner to pass out to people who ask questions. Here is my favorite:

> Elephant trainer Michael Hackenberger of the Bowmanville (Ontario) Zoo had his Tilley Hat snatched from his head and eaten by an elephant. *Three times.* Michael later would pick up his hat, wash it thoroughly, and wear it. He declined to accept a new one in order that we may have his well-travelled "Tilley" for our museum. *We are secretly pleased.*

"Teach Us to Pray"

Howard and Sue were part of the congregation where my family and I worshiped the previous five years in London. We learned to know each other well in a small-group Bible study. Howard is from a Jewish family, is an able scholar, and often brings a layer of understanding to the Scriptures that might otherwise escape a Gentile like me. Words of the Psalms and the Hebrew prophets flow readily from his lips during conversation, and he understands the Jewishness of Jesus' teaching.

The three of us made our way by bridge across a river of traffic at the M-25 motorway, and climbed gentle slopes to the top of the North Downs ridge. Below us we still could hear and see the busy beltway that carries commuters and commercial traffic around London every day. We sought out a quiet spot, protected from the cold wind, to read Luke 11:1-4:

[Jesus] was praying in a certain place, and after he had finished,
one of his disciples said to him, "Lord, teach us to pray, as John
taught his disciples." He said to them, "When you pray, say:
Father, hallowed be your name.
Your kingdom come.
Give us each day our daily bread.
And forgive us our sins,
for we ourselves forgive everyone indebted to us.
And do not bring us to the time of trial."

Prayer has been particularly important to Sue and Howard. I asked them about their understanding of prayer. Howard responded,

The disciples had to *ask* Jesus how they should pray. They didn't just naturally know. They had left everything to follow Jesus, and must have been feeling ghastly at the risk they had taken. So in the Lord's Prayer, Jesus taught them to pray, to rely on God. The first thing Jesus taught his disciples was to realize who God is. God is our Father, and that is not the main image Jews would have had of God. Of course, there are a few references to God as Father in the Psalms, but mostly the Jews thought of God as a Ruler and a King.

Images of God

I asked my companions what image of God comes to mind when they pray. "I pray to Jesus," Sue replied, "but Howard always prays to God. I have come to know God in Jesus."

Sue was putting into words a long-standing Christian belief: Jesus "is the image of the invisible God" and in him "all the fullness of God was pleased to dwell" (Col. 1:15, 19). God was in Christ, giving mortals an unparalleled view of who God is and how he relates to the world.

"Coming from a Jewish background," Howard said, "there was a time I screamed and rent my garments over someone praying to Jesus. I can see that God answers Susie's prayer. But I think her image of God is definitely more human than mine."

Our conversation had turned directly into one of the oldest puzzles of Christian faith: how could God, Creator of the universe, become visible in the form of a peasant from Galilee? The only way I can understand God being in Christ is to think that God chose to limit himself and to accept for a time the constraints of being human. One of the earliest hymns of the Christian church celebrates this extraordinary act on God's part. As recorded by Paul the apostle, the hymn speaks of "Christ Jesus, who,

> *though he was in the form of God,*
> *did not regard equality with God*
> *as something to be exploited,*
> *but emptied himself,*
> *taking the form of a slave,*
> *being born in human likeness.*
> *And being found in human form,*
> *he humbled himself*
> *and became obedient to the point of death*
> *—even death on a cross.* (Philippians 2:6-8)

When I think of God emptying himself to take on human flesh and serve as does a slave, that helps me understand what it means to consider Jesus as God. In the man from Galilee, we do not immediately recognize the full power and splendor of a God who hurls galaxies across distances measured in billions of light years. What we do see is the staggering love of a galaxy-hurling God who "emptied himself" of all such power, to live among us and experience the joy and pain of human existence.

Ways of Experiencing God

Christians experience God in a variety of ways: through biblical stories such as the liberation of Hebrew slaves from Egypt, through the teachings and life of Jesus, and through present-day encounters with a power that forgives sin, heals brokenness, and restores hope.

In early centuries of the Christian church, believers struggled to put these various ways of knowing God into an understandable explanation. The result was what we call the "Trinity" or the "three-in-one." There is no suggestion in this explanation that God is a committee! But humans know God as the Father who ceaselessly creates and protects, as the Son who lived and lives within history, and as the Holy Spirit who mystically fills our hearts with the wind and fire of divine love today.

Howard shared his experience and perspective,

> I don't see anything in my mind at all when I pray except light. For me, God is an extraordinary intensity of character and will. Jesus had that kind of formidable intensity of purpose. He was God's Word and God's will in flesh; he was a picture of God. Jesus wanted to demonstrate by his actions what God was doing in the world. That intensity of purpose gives me courage and makes me feel like a two-year-old with a very big daddy!

At this comment, Howard's laughter echoed back from the surrounding trees.

Like Howard, I usually pray simply to God rather than to Jesus. If I always prayed to Jesus, it would feel as though I were limiting my encounter with God to one-third of the Trinity. When I pray, I long to know the God who brought Hebrew slaves out of Egypt, the God who in Jesus turned water into wine, the God who at Pentecost transformed huddled and scared disciples

Sue and Howard Moss

into fearless missionaries. I want to worship the God who is Creator, Friend, and "rushing mighty wind" (Acts 2:2, KJV).

I often begin to pray with the words "Dear God," and finish with "in Jesus' name. Amen." There are countless images and characteristics of God from the Bible and elsewhere to put in between those two ways of addressing the Three-in-One. Most often I pray in silence, sensing and hungering for God rather than trying to fill the time with my own words.

Addressing God as Loving Parent

As we made our way eastward, we came to a high point in the Downs where we could look both north and south. On the far horizon to our left were the tallest buildings of London. To our right were the South Downs in the misty distance. We marveled at the beauty around us, and at the God who made this.

As we took in the view, Howard mused, "Prayer is like being the two-year-old child of a great emperor. You know most people are afraid of him, but he's your father. He loves you and provides for you."

In these words Howard caught something foundational to how we approach God in prayer. Our God created the wonders nearby and unseen worlds we cannot even imagine. But Jesus taught us to address this great God as "Abba"—the common household term for "father" in Jesus' native Aramaic language. It was the intimacy and warmth of Jesus' prayer to God that startled and transformed his disciples.

"Sometimes I experience God very intensely, much as I experience art," Sue said. She is an able artist who worked for a number of years as an illustrator at a museum in London. In any great piece of art, Sue explained, there is something of symbol and significance that is deeper than mere words can express.

Much of what I experience of God in prayer is similar. Words sometimes are important in prayer, but often I become aware of God through symbol, taste, sound, and touch. Jesus said, "I am the bread of life," and "I am the light of the world." His teaching about God enlisted all five senses. So I have learned that prayer can meaningfully involve more than words.

Establishing a Routine of Prayer

At the London Mennonite Centre in the previous five years, I had joined others twice a day for prayer. We entered the little chapel in silence, and sat on chairs or knelt on prayer stools in a semicircle around a table where a single candle burned. The candle reminded me that Jesus is the light of the world. By focusing my eyes on the flame, I would find my thoughts focusing in what God had done in Christ, and I would begin to pray.

Our prayer time always included a reading of Scripture, followed by a period of silence to reflect on what we had heard. Although there usually was a brief liturgy and spontaneous spoken prayers, I often felt God most present in the silence. If our prayers are always full of spoken words, when do we listen to God?

Howard began to quote from a portion of the Psalms where the writer describes the joy of people whose

delight is in the law of the Lord,
and on his law they meditate day and night.
They are like trees planted by streams of water,
which yield their fruit in its season,
and their leaves do not wither. (Psalm 1:2-3)

"Trees in the rain forest have shallow roots," Howard said. "They don't have to put down deep roots because there's always moisture at the surface. But a Middle Eastern date or a palm tree, in a semiarid climate, has to have deep roots." The same is true in our spiritual lives. There will be arid times when the water of God's presence seems absent or when hardship whips around us like a hurricane.

For Howard, "deep roots" has meant passionate prayer and reflection on the Scriptures:

My adversity has been illness—physical and emotional. My brain chemistry and adrenal system don't work right. Sometimes I have panic attacks, and I once spent a month in a psychiatric hospital. I live on a disability pension. Before all this happened, I was advancing in my academic profession at Cambridge, being a jolly clever boy. Everybody thought I would go far. Then my health collapsed—I had lived too long on adrenaline.

My academic work had been the most important thing to me, and then my health was taken away. That helplessness forced me to sort out priorities; I had to rely on God. Now my family and other relationships take high priority. I am not caught up with status and money, having no time for people I care about.

Cut Back to Produce More Fruit

At this point in the conversation, we approached one of several vineyards along the Pilgrims' Way. Howard continued his explanation of prayer, using the vine as an example. "I have seen vineyards that were nothing but little woody stumps; the vines had been cut right down to the ground. It hurts to be cut back, but sometimes that's how God makes us produce fruit." I asked what kind of fruit he was speaking of, and Howard replied, "Greater humanity and a real caring for weak people." The words of Jesus, in which he describes the relationship between himself and his disciples, came to mind:

> *I am the true vine, and my Father is the vinegrower. He removes every branch in me that bears no fruit. Every branch that bears fruit he prunes to make it bear more fruit. . . . Just as the branch cannot bear fruit by itself unless it abides in the vine, neither can you unless you abide in me. . . . If you keep my commandments, you will abide in my love, just as I have kept my Father's commandments and abide in his love. I have said these things to you so that my joy may be in you, and that your joy may be complete. (John 15:1-11)*

To "abide" in Jesus includes being in his presence through prayer and worship. The New Testament tells of many people who became disciples of Jesus after his death and resurrection, through some visual or spiritual encounter with Christ. I cannot imagine how dreary Christian discipleship would be without some awareness of that living presence.

Simply taking up the ethical teaching of Jesus, without his living companionship, would be a hard task. Many Christians experience short or long periods of Christ's seeming absence, but are sustained by memory of times when divine presence was unmistakable. They also are nurtured by continuing to worship with a faith community. Psalm 22 (quoted by Jesus on the cross) begins, "My God, my God, why have you forsaken me?" Later lines in the same psalm suggest that the wounded author remained in fellowship with believers:

> *From you comes my praise in the great congregation;*
> *my vows I will pay before those who fear him. . . .*
> *Those who seek him shall praise the Lord.* (Ps. 22:25-26)

We become aware of the living Christ in a variety of ways: reading about him in the Bible, reflecting on his teaching, speaking to him in prayer as we would to a friend, breaking bread in his memory, or hearing him through the voice of fellow Christians and even strangers. It is possible to get so busy and distracted with life that we lose an awareness of Christ walking with us. It takes discipline to set aside times of silence and listening when we become aware of the companion who gives us inner strength, forgiveness, reassurance, and unwavering love.

Yet, following Jesus cannot simply be an inner spiritual journey that makes us feel good about ourselves. To "abide in the vine" also means ordering our lives according to the example and teaching of Jesus. "If you keep my commandments, you will abide in my love," Jesus said. Obedience to Christ and being rooted in his love can never be separated.

Discipleship usually is not a grand calling or a spectacular act of martyrdom. Rather, it is a set of Christlike instincts and reflexive responses of love that gradually take shape in our lives over a period of years. We immerse ourselves in Scripture and in awareness of his presence. Then, when we have to respond quickly to a life situation, we are more likely to act in a way that is a credit to our Lord.

Love That Opens the Door

Howard and Sue have a modest apartment in a large London apartment block that houses many people with financial or social need. Time and again they have been hospitable and generous to others—to a friend who had spent several years in prison for assault, to a foreign student who struggled through a degree program and needed help in mastering the English language, and to people in need whom they met on the street.

Every two weeks for nearly twenty years, Sue helped coordinate worship and fellowship with a dozen individuals who were so mentally ill they could not sit through conventional church services. Howard worked with inner-city street people in London, many of whom were alcoholics or drug addicts. "We tried to get them detoxed, and to keep them from getting arrested for loitering," Howard said. "Many of those people had pancreatitis and mental illness. We prayed that God would heal them—and some were healed."

I marveled at Howard and Sue's love for others despite their own meager resources and bouts of illness. Howard recalled the story in Matthew (25:31-46) about people of the world facing judgment before Christ at the end of time. Eternal fellowship with God at that point will depend upon how we treated the Christ who came to us in the need and suffering of others.

Paraphrasing Christ's response to those who were indifferent to suffering, Howard imagined how some of today's Christians might protest: "'Lord, we *held marches* in your name! We started *radio stations* in your name!' Jesus will say, 'But I was hungry, and you gave me no food; I was thirsty and you gave me nothing to drink.' "

The kind of love that really cares for others in need is a rare thing, even among people who claim the love of Christ. "If you look at the Crusades and the harm that's been done in the name of Jesus, it's pretty depressing," Sue said. "But when you look at Jesus himself, he's compelling."

Howard agreed: "When you really see Jesus for who he is, you fall in love. You cannot bear to be without him."

A Heart to Care for Creation

As we talked, our footpath approached the back of a sloppy huddle of shacks and mobile homes. The ground was littered with trash, and we had to get around a big sign that said "Footway Closed." Most distressing was a skinny pony with its head hung listlessly out of a tumbledown barn. The footpath passed within yards of the barn, and we could see the pony's ribs and

Sue and Howard Moss offer a horse an apple from their lunch. This was not the mistreated horse we saw in the tumbledown barn.

dull coat of hair. The barn had not been cleaned out for a long time, and the pony stood on a deep bed of manure.

Sue and Howard were on the verge of tears, angry at the abuse of a pony and at the attitude someone has toward God's creation. "Look at how we humans care for our world!" said Howard. "Why do people wreck the environment? Why do people abuse animals? Why do people abuse children? There is evil in the world; it's as though we are witnessing the aftermath of some great disaster or nuclear war."

"Some day," Howard continued, "Jesus will return, and he'll destroy what cannot or will not be healed. Evil will cease to be. God gives us great inner peace now. But still there are children dying, and there is war."

The evil of someone abusing a pony along our footpath was just a tiny glimpse of the suffering and sin that devastate so much of the world. Hope and energy to respond to such brokenness may be hard to sustain. This is another reason for prayer. If we cannot even change ourselves without the power of God, it's unlikely we will change the world.

A Foot in Two Worlds

In late afternoon we left the Pilgrims' Way and walked along a blacktopped road into the village of Oxted. As we trudged under a railway bridge, a half dozen schoolboys about age fourteen passed us, headed the opposite direction. Howard was walking behind me and watched their response to my pilgrim attire.

"I could tell they were just resisting the temptation to make a comment about you," Howard said later with a big laugh (taking the Mickey out of me yet again). "But perhaps they resisted because you're a pretty big guy!"

My bed-and-breakfast that night was at a house that stands on the Prime Meridian, a north-south imaginary line that runs from the North Pole to the South Pole through Greenwich. It

Howard and Sue entering the village of Oxted

marks the point where each new calendar day begins on this spinning globe.

My congenial host took me out by the tulip bed where I could stand with one foot on either side of the invisible line. Standing with one foot in each of two worlds felt a bit like what it means to be a Christian.

The way of Jesus often is quite different from the accepted behavior and values in wider society. Christians have one foot in the kingdom of God and yet live in another world that has been warped by sin. We want to maintain balance, with a foot in two different worlds, and yet remaining faithful to the way of Jesus. That may require us to pray often with our eyes open!

Prayer

Dear God, I'm sometimes overwhelmed by the scale of emotional, spiritual, and physical need just in my own neighborhood. Beyond this neighborhood lies a world where children starve and nations destroy each other. Let me never forget or ignore that reality. Teach me how to pray, how to see clearly my own need for you. Let me empty myself of the need to succeed, and fill me with a passion for your kingdom. Teach me to give like Jesus gave, joyfully and freely. Amen.

For Reflection

1. What images do you have of God? As Father? Mother? Judge? Friend? Disciplinarian? Physician? Light? Why do you suppose Jesus wanted to teach his disciples to pray to God as "Father"?

2. What did it mean for Jesus to "empty himself"? What might that mean for you?

3. Do you pray to one person of the Trinity (Father, Son, and Holy Spirit) or just to "God"? In what ways is your language for God affected by your circumstance or the nature of your prayer?

4. In what ways has God "pruned" you like a vinedresser cuts back vines? What effect has such pruning had on your spiritual life?

5. How do you experience the tension of living with feet in two different worlds (the kingdom of God and the kingdom of the world)? How would it change your attitude toward the two if you believed God intends someday to make the two kingdoms one?

5

Feast Along the Way

Tuesday, May 21: Oxted to Otford (11 miles)
Fellow pilgrim: Will Newcomb

*The kingdom of God is like a banquet with a surprising list
of invitees • Disciples of Jesus celebrate the joy of community now
and the hope of a new creation in the future • We experience
salvation even in the midst of a world that suffers
from sin and violence • Values of the kingdom of God
already shape how we engage the world around us.*

Consecrated Ground

My bed-and-breakfast hosts at Oxted spared no effort to make
me comfortable. My meal in the morning was sumptuous: eggs,
mushrooms, bacon, toast, orange juice, four types of jam on an
elegant platter, parsley, and sausage ("the same kind the prime
minister likes best, from Smithfield Market"). Sunshine flooded
the dining room as I feasted, and classical music drifted in from
the kitchen. My heart was full of gratitude. Soon my stomach
was full enough to take me well into a day of walking.

Will Newcomb, a colleague of mine from the London Mennonite Centre, appeared at Oxted train station, and we walked
together to the village church nearby. Will was trained as an en-
gineer, worked in South Africa for a while, and now manages a
Christian mail-order book service. He is an accomplished ice-

The Oxted village church

skater, and he served for several years as an elder at the Mennonite congregation that began at the London Mennonite Centre.

Near a gate into the church grounds, a small sign announced,
"Consecrated ground; please clean up after your dog." We
laughed, walked by aged tombstones, and entered the nine-hun-
dred-year-old building to pray. Quietly we sat near the front. At
my feet a burial inscription was etched into gray stone:

> *Here Lyeth the Body of George Bond Esq*
> *The only Son of George Bond*
> *Who dyed the 22nd of Sept 1712*
> *In the 41st Year of his Age*

I couldn't help but think that I was forty-one, and often too
busy with life to think much about mortality. But by age forty,
anyone has seen enough of life to know there are times of dis-

couragement, loss, and depression. Together Will and I read our
assigned psalm for the day. It was a poem written by people in
misfortune who remembered an earlier occasion when God restored them to laughter and plenty:

> *When the Lord restored the fortunes of Zion,*
>   *we were like those who dream.*
> *Then our mouth was filled with laughter,*
>   *and our tongue with shouts of joy;*
>   *then it was said among the nations,*
>   *"The Lord has done great things for them."*
> *The Lord has done great things for us,*
>   *and we rejoiced.*
> *Restore our fortunes, O Lord,*
>   *like the watercourses in the Negeb.*
> *May those who sow in tears reap with shouts of joy.*
> *Those who go out weeping, bearing the seed for sowing,*
>   *shall come home with shouts of joy,*
>   *carrying their sheaves.* (Psalm 126)

Feasting and Discipleship

It may seem odd to consider feasting as a part of Christian discipleship. Yet even a quick reading of the Gospels reveals how
much time Jesus spent at table. Jesus admitted that he came "eating and drinking," and some uncharitable acquaintances accused him of being "a glutton and a drunkard, a friend of tax collectors and sinners!" (Luke 7:34).

It would not have been in character for Jesus to abuse his
body or to waste food, but it's clear that Jesus knew how to have
a good time. He was full of passion and wit, even if he had serious agenda. He told stories that held the attention of young and
old, related to all kinds of colorful and dubious characters, and
went to places that respectable people avoided. He turned water
into wine so a wedding party could carry on celebrating.

Jesus described salvation with the imagery of a great banquet:

*Someone gave a great dinner and invited many. At the time for
the dinner he sent his slave to say to those who had been invited,
"Come; for everything is ready now." But they all alike began to
make excuses. The first said to him, "I have bought a piece of
land, and I must go out and see it; please accept my regrets." Another said, "I have bought five yoke of oxen, and I am going to
try them out; please accept my regrets." Another said, "I have just
been married, and therefore I cannot come."*

*So the slave returned and reported this to his master. Then the
owner of the house became angry and said to his slave, "Go out
at once into the streets and lanes of the town and bring in the
poor, the crippled, the blind, and the lame." And the slave said,
"Sir, what you ordered has been done, and there is still room."
Then the master said to the slave, "Go out into the roads and
lanes, and compel people to come in, so that my house may be
filled. For I tell you, none of those who were invited will taste my
dinner."* (Luke 14:16-24)

A Community That Eats Together

One of the first things to impress Will about the Mennonite
congregation in London was the lunch the members frequently
share on Sunday noon. The meals are simple, with participants
each bringing a dish or a bit of fruit or some other food to place
on the table.

Once a month the members gather on Tuesday evenings for a
"fellowship communion." On that occasion someone makes a
batch of baked potatoes, and others bring salad, cheese, and top-
pings for the potatoes. The Lord's Supper then becomes a real
meal.

Will shared about what the church means for him:

Will Newcomb

When I first visited our church ten years ago, I had just been through some painful life experiences. I was depressed, and our shared lunches were a healing time. There was acceptance, not too many demands, and freedom to be myself.

It was such a contrast to the formal Christmas dinners with well-dressed and polite people I'd been to as a child, where people related on a superficial level. This was real community with people who shared deeply of their life experience, who were bound together by something stronger than blood ties. People were at home, enjoying themselves.

Feasting as an image for discipleship can mean more than just food. Jesus said about his followers, "I have come that they may have life, and have it abundantly" (John 10:10). Jesus made it clear that following him would require sacrifice and a willingness to suffer. But paradoxically, abundant life is also part of Christian discipleship.

The author of Hebrews captured something of the paradox when he wrote that Jesus, "for the sake of the joy that was set before him, endured the cross" (Hebrews 12:2). The Christians who have most inspired me have been people who have a deep sense of joy, even when life sometimes has been very painful.

Celebrating the Liberation to Come

On the night before he died, Jesus celebrated a Passover meal with his disciples. It commemorated the time God freed the Hebrew people from slavery in Egypt (Exodus 12). That was the meal when Jesus gave new meaning to the Passover bread and cup, calling them his body and blood.

Jesus also turned the meal into a time of expectation for the day when God would liberate all of creation from sin, death, and suffering. He said he would not eat a Passover meal again "until the kingdom of God comes," and urged his disciples to eat bread and drink wine "in remembrance of me" (Luke 22:18-19).

A meal among Christians is an opportunity to remember the price Jesus paid in his blood for our sin. It also reminds us that following Jesus means being willing to take up our own cross if discipleship gets us into social or political trouble. Then we look ahead with joy and confidence to the time when the peace of God's kingdom will fill the earth.

Perhaps the greatest reason Christians have to feast and celebrate is because we know that history makes sense: God has a purpose for both the world and our individual lives. The Bible has a story line that runs from the garden of Eden (creation; Genesis 2) through accounts of suffering and violence when humans rebel against our Creator (Genesis 3ff.). It proceeds to the coming of Jesus and God's plan to make a "new creation" (2 Corinthians 5:17).

What happened in this world history also happens with each individual: God creates us good, we rebel by trying to run our

own lives, and we need the power of God to make us new creatures.

Such a pattern of loss and renewal is not difficult to observe
in the physical world. People try to explain the origins of life and
the universe in various ways. Yet anyone can recognize times
and places when a pristine and well-ordered part of the world
was wrecked by greed or violence. We pollute rivers, destroy nations in war, and drive animals or plants to extinction. What
God created good we sometimes abuse and destroy. Paul had a
clear sense of both individuals and creation as a whole needing
to be restored:

> *The creation waits with eager longing for the revealing of the
> children of God; for the creation was subjected to futility, not of
> its own will but by the will of the one who subjected it, in hope
> that the creation itself will be set free from its bondage to decay
> and will obtain the freedom of the glory of the children of God.
> We know that the whole creation has been groaning in labor
> pains until now; and not only the creation, but we ourselves, who
> have the first fruits of the Spirit, groan inwardly while we wait
> for adoption, the redemption of our bodies.* (Romans 8:19-23)

Paul pictures all of the physical and spiritual world as aching
for signs of hope. He particularly sees hope in men and women
who once again acknowledge God as Father. "Creation waits
with eager longing for the revealing of the children of God."

Creation has been "subjected to futility." God has allowed his
world to suffer the ill effects of being under the domination of
people and powers who do not share God's passion for healing
and wholeness. The resulting chaos, violence, and destruction
bring the world to a state of agony like a woman in difficult
childbirth.

Into this pain God brings hope and new life, and something
of a renewed creation already happens in our lives. We have the

"first fruits of the Spirit," the beginning of a tide of forgiveness and restoration that someday will cover the earth.

Finding Security in God

Early in his Christian experience, Will Newcomb felt a yearning to see the love of Jesus speak to the violence, fear, and hatred generated by nuclear weapons. This was in the 1980s, when there was talk of nuclear war, when tension ran high between the Soviet Union and Western Europe. The British government permitted American cruise missiles to be stationed in England, and Will joined other Christians to protest at the missile bases. He said,

> Jesus needed to be visible there as well as in my church. Even some Christians seemed to rely on military technology for security. Yet already in the early years of Jewish history, God had told his people *he* was their security. God told the Israelites to burn captured chariots and hamstring the horses (Joshua 11:6); they were not to have the same weaponry as their enemies. They were to be exposed and vulnerable, seemingly defenseless in the eyes of their enemies (Deut. 20:1-4). God would protect and save them.

The text from Deuteronomy that Will cited goes on to describe God's people engaging in military battles (though without the advanced weaponry of their foes). These sometimes led to the slaughter of other peoples. In contrast, the example and teaching of Jesus raise the notion of trusting in God to a new level. Even when Jesus was betrayed, tried, and crucified, he was able to love and forgive those who sought to harm him.

The transforming power of God's love in Jesus was so great that he was willing to lose his own life for the greater good of showing a new way to confront evil. Jesus relied on the power of

God to overcome the forces of hatred, a power that became most evident in the resurrection.

That kind of trust in God is a deep expression of worship. Will realized that confronting the evil of nuclear weapons would also be an act of worship. On several occasions, he joined other Christian protesters outside military bases to pray that God's love would reach the soldiers guarding the bombs. He reported,

> We sought God's forgiveness for the way nations were turning their backs on him and lifting up the "golden calf" of mutually assured destruction. We broke bread together while Vulcan bombers roared across the sky with cavernous bomb bays open during an air display. We laid a large wooden cross in the snow outside the Ministry of Defence building in London on Ash Wednesday. We wrote prayers of repentance for ourselves and our country and nailed them to the cross.

Face-to-Face with Violence

Perhaps a commitment to loving political enemies seems easy in a stable, democratic country where there usually is little physical danger. But during the time of his witness at military bases, Will had a sudden opportunity to address a situation of violence on a very personal level.

> One New Year's Eve, at midnight, a friend and I were driving through London and came across a fourteen-year-old Asian boy being beaten up by a large white man. We stopped the car and ran over to do something about it. The boy had a group of friends nearby, but they were too terrified to get involved. The man kept jumping up and down on the kid's head. By the time we reached him, the attacker had run off, and the unconscious boy was being dragged away by his friends.

Since they refused to let him lie still and wait for an ambulance, I persuaded them to get into our car and I'd drive them to the hospital. By the time we got to the car, though, the madman was back. He punched the woman with me, broke her cheekbone, and then started laying into me. It seemed like the boy was the most vulnerable person in that situation, so as I fell, I grabbed him so he'd be protected by my body.

With my head getting kicked in, and feeling a boot crunch into my back again and again, it seemed like the ideal time to pray! With every ounce of strength I cried, "Jesus save me!" Almost at once the attacker ran off, taking a few more swipes at people along the way. We jumped into the car, locked the doors, and turned on the ignition switch. With our headlights on and the engine revving, the attacker stopped dead. I could have run him over and pinned him down with car—but I did not. Then he ran off.

Will reflected on the reasons he got involved.

Did I do the right thing? My friend has since decided that the next time, she will run and phone the police. I hope I would still go in and try to protect the person getting hit. Jesus calls me to be involved in the world. I should not just pass by and let others respond to the situation. I'd want someone to come to my aid if I were the focus of an attack. Jesus said, "Do to others as you would have them do to you." (Luke 6:31)

Like Being in Love

I asked Will what brought him to such a deep commitment to the way of Jesus. He responded,

As a young man, with two other friends I sailed a yacht from England to the Caribbean. Often I was at the helm on the night-to-morning watch. Each dawn the sky slowly changed from black to a touch of blue, then to red, then to orange—and finally the sun rose.

During that Atlantic crossing, I was away from my usual world for twenty-three days. I started to wonder how it all got started and whether God cared about me. I was seeking God. When I eventually got to the United States and did some traveling, I kept meeting people who took me in and showed hospitality. I had a sense that Someone cared and was looking after me.

In America, Will met a Christian woman who took him to the airport when he returned to England. She asked Will if he wanted to know Jesus. Will told me,

My life at that time was going pretty well, but I had an awareness of sin. I wanted God to forgive me and fill me. My friend prayed with me, and gave me a pocket New Testament, which I read on the airplane. I gave my life to Jesus, and had an experience of the living God. I felt his love and forgiveness in a tangible way, as if Jesus was holding me in a warm, healing embrace. It was a bit like being in love—you know it deep in your bones, and it changes the direction of your life. I knew I was not alone.

The delight with which Will described his coming to faith matched the environment in which we walked and talked. It was the most beautiful weather of my journey so far, with sky as blue as the sea and clouds as white as freshly washed linens.

At noon, Will and I stopped in a meadow carpeted with dandelions, pulled sandwiches from our bags, and watched a thunderstorm blow across the hills far in the distance. A great bolt of lightning momentarily bridged heaven and earth, followed by the distant rumble of thunder. Nearby a calf was repeatedly launching off the ground with all four legs, as though spring-loaded, apparently just for sheer pleasure.

Giving Up an Old Religion

Will continued to reflect on the changes that happened when he became a Christian. "I had to give up my old religion of small boat racing." He laughed. "The sailing club had become an obsession for me, the place I spent most of my weekends. When I became a Christian, I didn't even give it a second thought. Now I wanted my best energies apart from a regular job to be in the life and mission of the church."

I asked Will if he had to give up anything else besides boat racing to follow Jesus. He answered,

I gave up some of my sense of independence and gained a community where I belonged. I was nurtured by group prayer at church and in a home group that met each week. What we had in common was our commitment to Jesus. That freed each of us to reveal more of ourselves. In the presence of God, there is freedom to be known, and I discovered I didn't have to hide. When I pray with other Christians, I feel a sense of security even with people I don't know very well.

The Transforming Power of Total Commitment

In the year before Will and I walked together, he was dating and considering the possibility of marriage. Some friends recommended that he and his girlfriend live together as lovers to test whether the relationship could last. Will rejected that idea, understanding sexual intimacy as part of a lifelong commitment, not as something for a trial relationship.

"A friend of mine had a live-in boyfriend, and eventually married him," Will said. "She told me how different it was to have made a commitment to each other. A life-changing relationship is not something you can achieve with partial commitment."

The same is true for following Jesus, I thought. Either our lives are directed toward the kingdom of God, or they are not. One cannot build a viable marriage by picking and choosing which parts of life belong to a partner. Likewise, we cannot come to know God by bargaining to keep career or leisure time or money to ourselves; it all belongs to God.

This doesn't mean we spend all or even most of our time with other Christians when we follow Jesus. God called Will to abandon his sailing passion, but might call others to stay with a sailing club and share the love of Jesus in that setting. Will now does that at an ice-skating club.

Although my work in recent years has been mostly in the church, I have always had close friends who are not believers. That's because I enjoy being with interesting people regardless of their faith commitment, and I have learned a lot about life from nonbelievers. I also want to keep some perspective on what the church looks like to people outside the church. It's too easy for faith to become stuffy and distant from the concerns of people who do not know Jesus. Besides, I would have no opportunity to invite others to faith if I only related to those who already are committed.

Clouds swept in from the horizon, and rain spilled from the heavens in bucketfuls as Will and I approached the village of Otford. We sought refuge at a crooked fifteenth-century inn, then carried on to the train station when the drenching subsided.

A Eurostar train eased along the tracks on its way to Paris via the new Channel tunnel. Before boarding a train going the other direction, Will gave me a hug and a blessing. Then I walked back through the village again, holding in hand the address of my overnight lodging.

A Dilemma of Loyalties

At the edge of town, my hosts owned a lovely old hops barn (also called an "oast house"), which they had converted into a residence. Hops is a flowering plant used in the production of traditional ales, a common crop in southeast England. A hops barn has a large, round, squat brick section with a cone-shaped roof, in which the hops flowers are dried over fire.

Adjacent to that structure is a rectangular barn used for cooling and storing the finished product. On top of the cone-shaped roof is a revolving hood that turns in the wind like a giant weather vane, allowing an updraft while protecting the drying hops from rain.

A young man name Mark, also a guest, was reading in the sitting room when I arrived at the hops barn. We fell into conversation, and I learned he was a master's student in physics at a British university. He already had been living at the hops barn for two weeks while he worked temporarily at the military re-

Typical oast houses in southeastern England. Once used to dry hops, the buildings on this photo have been converted into dwellings.

Mark, in front of the ruins of Otford Palace

search laboratories on a hilltop overlooking Otford. He asked politely about my activities, and I explained that I was writing a book on Christian discipleship.

"I'm a Christian," he said warmly, and we talked for a while about what it means to follow Jesus. The sky had cleared again, and the late evening sun angled across the village. We walked half a mile to the ruins of the medieval Otford Palace. A historical marker at the ruins explained that until 1537 the palace had been one of a chain of houses belonging to the Archbishops of Canterbury.

"People in this culture don't like to talk about religion," Mark observed. "We're not so much an atheist state as an embarrassed state. For centuries the church was so politically powerful that people were indoctrinated into a way of believing. Now that religion isn't forced upon the population any more, many people are glad not to have anything to do with the church."

Mark explained that he was raised in a Christian family, but he didn't make a personal commitment to Christ until he was twenty. I asked whether being a Christian had any bearing on his work at the military laboratory. He pondered a moment, then answered thoughtfully, "I'm not working for a department of war, but for a department of defense. I've always been a pacifist, and I don't want to hurt anybody. I do have reservations about my work. The Bible says, 'Love your neighbor as yourself.' "

Here I interjected that Jesus calls us to love even our enemies.

Mark nodded and said, "I have to ask, will my work at the laboratory be directly involved in killing people? I work on optics, and if I'm designing a lens that is used to take pictures in order to kill someone, then am I showing love?"

Tension Between the Gospel and Our World

Mark was struggling with the tension many Christians feel between lofty standards of the gospel and quite different values in secular society. What if a good job is available in the "defense" industry, even though Jesus calls us to love our enemies? How much can Christians be involved in such a setting before we have compromised our commitment to follow Jesus?

Mark's dilemma is parallel to other circumstances where Christians may be expected to act in ways that are difficult to reconcile with the Jesus of the Gospels. What do we do if a supervisor at work wants us to lie for the company? What if money we put into a retirement plan gets used to manufacture land mines?

It is worth considering in advance how we might respond to such dilemmas. The value of immersing ourselves in Scripture is that it shapes our reflexes and attitudes. Suppose we decide in advance that the call to follow Jesus means having nothing to do with using or making instruments of war. Then a military job will be ruled out from the start.

If we resolve always to follow Jesus' teaching about truth-telling, then there is not much to decide when an employer expects us to lie. Taking a stance on such issues may be costly, and we will need the support of a Christian community to sustain such a way of discipleship. We will need the Holy Spirit in our lives, giving us power to live by different values and priorities.

I do not stand in judgment of Mark and his employment at a military laboratory. He is a student, this is part of his training, and he is asking questions about what his future employment will be. He is ready to talk with other Christians about the appropriateness of this work, and to measure his decisions against the Scriptures. I admired his openness and his determination to follow Jesus. Perhaps the *direction* of our lives is more important than the exact *position* we hold on a given issue. Are we moving toward the way of Jesus, or away from it?

A Place at the Worldwide Table

Having spent the day thinking about feasting, I couldn't help but consider what a military laboratory on the nearby hilltop represented in terms of food at the world table. I have heard many observers say that this earth easily could produce enough food to nourish every living person.

There is hunger and even starvation, though, because of war and because so many resources are used to develop and purchase weapons. Guns and bombs directly kill millions of people each year. Countless others slip into poverty because governments buy military hardware instead of investing in hospitals, schools, and food production.

In Western Europe or North America, we are scarcely aware of this, because we produce the weapons that poorer nations buy. We become wealthy in this arrangement, because the production of weapons creates jobs—though fewer jobs than if the same resources were put to nonmilitary purposes.

God's love for all of creation means it is not enough for me to enjoy my own feast or simply to eat my fill at the table of a local faith community. I also must care about the world table, doing what I can to help people of my own country "beat their swords into plowshares" (Isaiah 2:4).

Prayer

God of peace, thank you for making a place at your table for me. I long for a time when people with physical and spiritual hunger the world over will feast as sisters and brothers in the kingdom of God. Thank you for the signs of the kingdom that I already experience with followers of Jesus who share their lives in trust, mutual respect, and love. Help me to order my priorities so that I can contribute to the healing of creation. Amen.

For Reflection

1. Where or how have you seen signs of "abundant life" among followers of Jesus? Have there been specific people or experiences that showed you the joy of Christian community?

2. What signs do you see of creation "groaning" for liberation? Do you know of people or organizations that are addressing those painful circumstances?

3. What have you given up to follow Jesus? What have you gained?

4. Are there times in your life when loyalty to Jesus clashed with loyalty to something else that also attracted or demanded allegiance? How did you resolve the conflict?

Invest for the Kingdom

Wednesday, May 22: Otford to Strood (19 miles)
Fellow pilgrim: Noel Moules[1]

God's shalom *(peace) brings a life-encompassing wholeness
and well-being • God calls us to live in* shalom *wherever we are
and to share that with others • The values of* shalom *(justice, truth,
mercy) shape the vocational choices of disciples • God's love
and forgiveness free us from guilt when we fail to measure up
to demands of the gospel • Doubt can spur us to think critically
about our faith • Conversion is a lifelong process • We gain strength
by immersing ourselves in the Bible, seeking fellowship
with other believers, and finding a mentor to guide us.*

The *Shalom* Man

While eating breakfast at the hops house, I surveyed maps and realized I had made a miscalculation on mileage for the day's journey. Instead of the eleven miles I had promised my fellow pilgrim, we had almost twenty miles to go!

Just east of Otford, the North Downs Way diverges sharply from the Pilgrims' Way before crossing the River Medway, taking a more northerly and scenic route that adds seven or eight miles to the distance. I was happy to take this detour, and already had lodging arranged in that direction. But I had read mileage for the shorter route in the guidebooks when I calculated the distance.

How would I break this news to Noel Moules, my walking companion for the day?

"*Shalom,* Nelson!" Noel said with his customary burst of warmth when we met at the train station. The greeting came as no surprise. I had known Noel for five years as the "*shalom* man," since that Hebrew word for peace is daily on his tongue. Noel will be quick to tell you that the English word "peace" is not an adequate translation for biblical *shalom,* since people often use "peace" simply to mean an absence of war or obvious conflict.

Psalm 128 (our reading for the morning) is one of many examples where the Hebrew concept of *shalom*/peace means much more:

> *Happy is everyone who fears the Lord,*
> *   who walks in his ways.*
> *You shall eat the fruit of the labor of your hands;*
> *   you shall be happy, and it shall go well with you. . . .*
> *The Lord bless you from Zion.*
> *May you see the prosperity of Jerusalem*
> *   all the days of your life.*
> *May you see your children's children.*
> *Peace be upon Israel!*

The Hebrews used *shalom*/peace to mean a general condition of well-being, plenty, security, justice, and belonging. Above all, *shalom* has to do with relationships: being in harmony with our Creator, relating wisely to the physical world, and building bridges of mutual respect with other people. For Noel, *shalom* is the "secret of the universe," the God-designed way in which all things someday will fit together.

A Metamorphosis of the Spirit

If the government ever put a special tax on exuberance, Noel would have to pay a fortune. Until that happens, he is free to

Noel Moules

lavish upon friends his good humor and passionate delight in knowing Jesus.

I was surprised to learn, as we trudged up a hill behind Otford, that Noel was introspective and withdrawn as a child. "Then at age nineteen I had an experience of the Holy Spirit," he said, "and was set free. I had a metamorphosis of the Spirit."

I didn't know Noel as a child, but at age fifty he is a walking reservoir of spiritual insight and zest for life. "Workshop," the yearlong Christian leadership training program he founded and directs, has had more than two and a half thousand participants across Britain. Noel works hard, and once told me with a glint in his eye that he intends to live to be 120. "Most men have a mid-life crisis in their forties. At sixty, I'm going to have a midlife cele-bration!"

At every turn in the path, Noel seemed to breathe in beauty from the surrounding woods and meadows. It was not a sunny or warm day. Yet Noel lives every moment intensely and misses no opportunity for enjoyment.

I asked him how he ended up settling in a crowded section of inner-city London.

Living in an urban environment is most unnatural for my wife, Rowena, and me. We're wilderness people. The words of the poet W. B. Yeats capture our love of the quiet natural tranquility of the sky, the water, and the earth as he speaks of the island of Innisfree:

> I will arise and go now,
>   and go to Innisfree,
> And a small cabin build there,
>   of clay and wattles made:
> Nine bean-rows will I have there,
>   a hive for the honey-bee,
> And live alone in the bee-loud glade.
> And I shall have some peace there.

Many years ago I felt God say to me, 'Noel, I want you to bring the *shalom* of the island of Innisfree to the urban envi-ronment.' Rowena and I have always worked to make our home in the city a place of peace and of deep *shalom*.

Investing in the Kingdom

I am fascinated by one so gifted as Noel choosing to invest his considerable ability in work that has not brought much financial security or prestige, as measured by society. Noel has taken up a strenuous and risky life calling. If you ask him about it, he points to the parable of the pounds (Luke 19:11-27).

In that story, Jesus describes how a nobleman gave a pound of money to each of ten slaves before he left on a long journey. When he returned, he summoned the slaves and asked them to account for what they had done with the money. One had invested his money and made ten more pounds; another had taken five and made five more. Both were given rule over a matching number of cities. Then another slave came forward:

> *"Lord, here is your pound. I wrapped it up in a piece of cloth, for I was afraid of you, because you are a harsh man; you take what you did not deposit, and reap what you did not sow." He said to him, "I will judge you by your own words, you wicked slave! You knew, did you, that I was a harsh man, taking what I did not deposit and reaping what I did not sow? Why then did you not put my money into the bank? Then when I returned, I could have collected it with interest."*

Noel carried on with his interpretation:

The master in that story gives money to each of his ten slaves and simply says, "Do business with this until I come back." The master grants complete freedom for them to find possibilities for investment and to use their ingenuity.

Noel recalled a time sixteen years earlier. He suddenly had the sense that he could design a discipleship training program in England that was not available in any other way. "I don't doubt that God planted that idea," Noel said, "but it was mine to nurture and develop."

What emerged from that inner call was a training course that participants attend for eleven full weekends throughout the course of a year, at three locations in England. Topics at Workshop cover everything from the "salvation landscape" of the Bible and church history to prophecy and the problem of evil. Noel does much of the teaching. He takes to that task like a gazelle takes to running.

There is power in the lives of men and women who invest their natural abilities in work God can bless and use to show his love. Surely God does not want everyone to be a teacher like Noel. The world also needs followers of Jesus in hospitals, factories, offices, daycare centers, and homes. But the message of Jesus' parable about investment is that everyone can find ways to deploy skills or abilities for the kingdom.

Some Christians keenly feel the hand of God guiding them to specific work. Others only become aware of divine guidance in retrospect. For them, decisions about career and vocation often seemed difficult and ambiguous at the time. Noel continued,

Following Jesus and developing a sense of vocation has nothing to do with rules, and everything to do with relationship and character. The trouble with rules is that they don't teach you to cope with a broad-enough set of possible circumstances. Discipleship and vocation are about values: we learn to work with Jesus' example.

We ask, "How would Jesus respond in a situation like this? What work might Jesus do with this set of gifts and opportunities?" People never knew what Jesus would do next, but paradoxically, he was always consistent. He was consistent by being centered in the Father, and he was unpredictable by living on the edge of society. He was disturbing and provocative, but also gentle and reassuring.

Instead of imposing some kind of new legalism, Jesus showed us how to live by a cascade of *values:* freedom, justice, truth, joy, mercy, and *shalom.* The prophet Amos said, "Let justice roll down like waters, and righteousness like an everflowing stream" (Amos 5:24). Jesus picked up that theme and said, "Out of the believer's heart shall flow rivers of living water" (John 7:38).

The Gospel of John goes on to explain that Jesus was talking about the Holy Spirit when he spoke of "living water" (7:39). It's a reminder that life-changing, Jesus-centered values do not just spring up by sheer will power. As followers of Jesus, we must tap into a source of power bigger than ourselves.

An Unintended Detour

So engrossed were Noel and I in our conversation that we neglected to read our map carefully, took a wrong turn, and got off the Pilgrims' Way. England is crisscrossed with more than a hundred thousand miles of public footpaths. Virtually every square mile of the country has one or more paths. The expectations are simple: keep to the marked path, respect property, close all gates behind you (so sheep or cattle don't get out), keep your dog on a leash during lambing season, and don't start fires.

A large part of the Pilgrims' Way stands out in the landscape as a well-defined road. But now Noel and I were on a leg of the journey where we had to follow a zigzag route through a labyrinth of possible footpaths.

Most of this stretch of the Pilgrims' Way was well-marked, but some of the waymarks got lost in undergrowth. We needed to compare the path with the map frequently and use a compass, but we had failed to do that for an hour. In the midst of a discussion about finding our way through the maze of life, we got thoroughly disoriented on the Pilgrims' Way.

We tried walking a mile down a muddy farm lane that spilled out onto a golf course. Groundskeepers scratched their heads and told us we were off the edge of our map. Eventually we re-traced that muddy mile, and I regretted the extra wear on our feet. This already was going to be the longest day of the walk, and by carelessness we just had added two sticky miles!

Our consolation was the bluebells, which flooded the surrounding woods as though a magical river had burst its banks. "If you painted a picture of this, people wouldn't believe you," Noel exclaimed. For the first time I lamented having only black-and-white film in my camera. "Even when you lose your way, you stumble upon miracles," Noel said with a broad smile.

This Is My Father's House

We stopped at the village of Wrotham to find a dry place for lunch. It was raining lightly, and we took shelter at the stone porch of St. George's Church. "Do you think it's okay to eat in here?" I asked.

"Of course." Noel laughed. "This is my Father's house." Not long after we began eating, Reverend Heather Turner, the village priest, came into the porch with a basket under her arm. It was dark in the porch passageway, and we startled her a bit. She re-covered quickly and inquired warmly who we were. We explained the nature of our journey.

"You are welcome, very welcome indeed," she said, then went into the church to make us a pot of tea.

"Angels come in many guises," Noel quipped, "even as vicars!"

We warmed our hands on hot teacups, thanked Reverend Turner for her kindness, and learned that she had been a nurse for twenty-six years before taking up her present role in the church. She was part of the first group of women ever ordained

Reverend Heather Turner, a vicar at St. George's church in Wrotham

to the ministry in the Church of England.

Shortly before meeting us she had read Psalm 23 at the deathbed of a ninety-five-year-old woman. With a mixture of sadness and peace on her face, Reverend Turner said to us, "One of the rich aspects of our faith is knowing that God will be there to meet us when we die." Then she disappeared into the church building, and we took her comments as a blessing.

Not wanting to lose time or get stiff sitting in the cool and damp, Noel and I pressed on in the rain. "Here we were talking this morning about using our gifts for God, and we meet a woman who at midlife finally has been able to use her gifts fully within the church," Noel said.

I recalled the time several years earlier when I was with a group of Christians gathered around a television set, waiting for results of a vote by Church of England leaders on the issue of women's ordination. Our joy at knowing women and men both now could provide leadership in that denomination was tempered by the reality that women for centuries virtually had been silenced in churches of most denominations.

Guilt from Demands of the Gospel

I commented on the fact that the church in the Western world sometimes has been a place of legalism and repression. Noel agreed:

Yes, and there's still a tremendous amount of guilt in the church. People feel caught between what they see as demands of the gospel and the shabby reality of their own lives. The liberating truth we have to understand is that we are *learning*, we are *disciples*, we haven't arrived. Jesus is our elder brother, and we "grow up in every way into him" (Ephesians 4:15).

We're like a child on the playground, looking at a big brother and saying, "Some day I'm going to be like him." I don't mean we should be childish or self-centered. But we should be childlike, following Jesus our Brother in wonder and trust. Childlikeness is wisdom and maturity that has grown up to become a child.

Here Noel broke out into a line from his favorite folk musician, Bob Dylan: "Ah, but I was so much older then, I'm younger than that now."

I shared a recent experience: One of my daughters came to me in tears, aware perhaps for the first time that she had done something that would displease God. "What if God doesn't forgive me?" she asked. "What if I died and had done something wrong, would I go to heaven?"

I held her and asked if she thought mom and I ever would put her out of the house and say we didn't love her, just because she had done something wrong.

"Of course not," she said with complete confidence.

"Then if we love you like that," I said, "as an ordinary mom and dad, how much more do you think God loves you?"

God loves and receives everyone who seeks him. We become children of God and followers of Jesus, not because we have a perfect track record of obedience, but because we have put ourselves into the arms of a God who loves and forgives.

Doubt Can Be a Good Thing

Along with feeling guilty about a failure to live up to the gospel, many Christians are afraid when they question basic beliefs of their own faith. Noel insisted that doubt can be a good thing. "If you never let hard questions ripple the surface of your soul, you're in a dangerous position. We live in a secular society, and we engage people around us who ask hard questions and challenge what we believe. Doubt can be destructive, but it can also be liberating. I have come to root my faith understanding in a *historical* Jesus, in a man who actually lived and taught and died and rose again almost two thousand years ago."

I asked how we can know for certain that Jesus is risen—the central conviction of Christian faith.

Noel pondered the question for a moment before replying. "It's a living relationship with Jesus that builds assurance. God hates religion, any mere code of beliefs and rules (such as, read the Bible every day, don't smoke) that give a pseudo-security. What God wants is *relationship,* and in Jesus such a relationship is possible in a new way."

In life-changing discipleship, there is a vital link between the historical Jesus and a living relationship with him in the present. We need our understanding of appropriate ways to live to be grounded in Jesus, who himself was grounded in God and the Hebrew Scriptures. If it isn't, we are tempted simply to relish the presence of God on a mystical level and let our daily lives go on unchanged. Or we are tempted to be Christians on Sunday (when we go to church) and live like anybody else the rest of the week.

Conversion over a Period of Years

"Becoming a Christian is not a short, quick experience," Noel said. A recent study of new believers in England revealed that most of them could not point to a specific day when they "became a Christian." Instead, conversion or change happened over a period of months or even years.

"Conversion means making a big change down in the engine room," Noel said. "It's not just changing things around up on the decks."

The well-known image of being "born again" is a biblical metaphor, and suggests a dramatic change at a given point in time. But that is only one of many biblical images of conversion, and there are others including "set free" and "redeemed" (bought back).

Paul the apostle variously says we "have been saved," we "are being saved," and we "will be saved." Conversion is a lifelong process that will only be complete when we die and live in the presence of God. Until then, we sometimes will struggle with doubt, discouragement, and sin.

Noel developed the theme of struggle further:

On the night before Jesus died, he said to Peter and the rest of the disciples, "Listen! Satan has demanded to sift all of you like wheat, but I have prayed for you that your own faith may not fail" (Luke 22:31). Such sifting by doubt or opposition is God's quality control.

Testing is a challenge to our stature as Christians. Jesus himself stands with us in the presence of the Holy Spirit.

There are three ways Noel suggested for followers of Jesus to grow strong and stand up in times of testing:

"First, Christians must learn to read, interpret, and understand the Scriptures." He noted that reading the Bible is not always an easy thing to do, since there sometimes is a great cultural gulf between the ancient world and modern society. New Christians in particular may need to find a church or some other setting where there is teaching that provides a basic introduction to books and themes of the Bible. It can be helpful to use a study Bible with an introduction to the individual books and footnotes that explain difficult or complex passages.

At this point I recalled the puzzlement of my Jewish fellow pilgrim, Howard Moss, during a conversation several days earlier. He was raised in a tradition in which people commit large portions of Scripture to memory. Howard once mentioned that he is startled to see that many Christians don't really know—let alone memorize—the Bible.

"Why don't Christians learn the teachings of their Rabbi [teacher]?" he once asked me with a touch of frustration.

Howard's question has burned in my ears, and over the last years I've committed to memory selections of the Old Testament prophets, the teachings of Jesus, and Paul's letters. To reinforce my memory, I usually read from the same English translation of the Bible. Phrases don't stay on my circuit board very long if I hear them three or four different ways.

I also have formed the habit of trying to memorize even a short bit of almost any biblical passage I read. I pick out a sentence or a few verses that speak to me, repeat them several times, then turn back to those verses over the following two or three days. Over a period of years, those scattered fragments of memorized Scripture become more numerous. Gradually they weave

The eastern stretch of the Pilgrims' Way often crosses a farmer's field.

a fabric of familiar texts, providing a spiritual resource that warms, comforts, and challenges.

"Second," Noel continued, "Christians must make time for fellowship with other Christians. The letter to the Hebrews says we should care for each other, 'not neglecting to meet together, . . . but encouraging one another' " (Hebrews 10:25). The church, as a community of faith, is the unique environment God has created in which we can grow in the life of the Spirit.

For Noel, Christian fellowship is the place of the "soul friend," another disciple or other disciples whose maturity, love, and wisdom help us become like Jesus. There is a long tradition of "spiritual direction" in the church, in which a person of spiritual stature regularly meets with another believer to encourage, provide guidance, and hear confession. People who don't want such a formal mentoring arrangement still could meet regularly with a trusted Christian friend to pray and to talk about what discipleship means on a day-to-day basis. Noel expanded on this point:

The biblical vision of the church is both global and local, and disciples of Jesus are part of both dimensions. The saying of our time, "think global, act local," is as significant for Christians as for anyone. Disciples choose freely to play their part in the local Christian community—not only to receive, but also to allow God to use their gifts and abilities to enrich others.

Participation in the church does not grow out of any legalism. Instead, it comes from the joyful freedom of choosing to work out the practical meaning of being part of the "body of Christ." Just as athletes need to train to reach peak fitness and ability, so we need to work out as a body to develop and sharpen our fitness.

Noel acknowledged that it is sometimes tough to work out the meaning of discipleship with others who share our faith but have different personalities:

Working through such differences makes fellowship a reality. We learn to serve one another. Jesus gave the example of washing other people's feet. Such service is true leadership. We are to "bear one another's burdens" (Galatians 6:2). We are to share the spiritual, emotional, and material support we all need. The New Testament word for such a level of mutual sharing is *koinonia* (often translated as "fellowship").

Third, it is essential for disciples of Jesus to have a big vision of what God is doing and will do. Some Christians have a narrow perspective, and don't see the significance of their lives in God's scheme of things. God calls us to live our lives under an open heaven, where Jesus has torn apart the barriers between the spiritual and the physical.

Under God's open heaven, we learn to see miracles in the details of our lives as a natural and everyday occurrence. We live our lives against the backdrop of God working out his purposes in cosmic terms. We become part of a vision of *shalom,* in which we see God drawing the whole universe together into perfect harmony and integrated, energized wholeness.

In this world, events can at times seem out of control. Yet there is wonderful freedom and joy in knowing that history is unfolding within a perfect plan of God. Noel said,

Such a way of seeing probably will not all come at once. It will need to be nurtured and developed by Scripture, teaching, and inspired encouragement from others. To know for a certainty that God is working everything out to bring into being a new heaven and earth is the most exciting thing in the world. God takes every day of our life, every action no matter how insignificant, and makes them part of his divine purpose.

Asked what his motto is, Noel responded with the words of the apostle Paul:

It is [Jesus Christ] whom we proclaim, warning everyone and teaching everyone in all wisdom, so that we may present everyone mature in Christ. For this I toil and struggle with all the energy that he powerfully inspires within me. (Colossians 1:28-29)

"All this is only because of the vision of *shalom* I have in my heart," Noel concluded. "I am simply like a child who has found the secret of the universe!"

Limping into Strood

It was late afternoon when we crossed a high ridge just before reaching the River Medway. A strong wind set in, and heavy clouds filled the valley ahead with deepening haze and fog. From an inner pocket of his jacket, Noel extracted a mobile telephone and gave his wife a quick update on our progress.

We finally entered the town and plodded wearily uphill toward my lodging on Watling Street (the road along which Chaucer's pilgrims traveled in medieval times). The last long street, after nineteen miles, felt like the biggest hill of the day. "Are you *travelers* [Gypsies]?" a group of teenage boys taunted from across the street.

"Yes!" we answered, and laughed.

We had expected that Noel could get a bus from Watling Street to the train station in nearby Rochester. But the last buses on that route had already run. There was one-third of a mile for

Noel to walk yet to make a bus connection. I watched him disappear down the street in the gloom and damp. He was limping, and I did the same as I approached the door of my bed-and-breakfast lodging.

Prayer

Lord, I want my gifts and abilities to be put to use for your kingdom. Show me how I can invest the talents you give me in service to you and others. Thank you that your love and mercy are larger than my failures. Forgive my sin, and free me from guilt that could take away joy. Let your shalom transform my life so profoundly that I can be an agent of healing and reconciliation to others. I bring my questions and doubts to you as part of my desire to know you with heart and mind. Give me soul friends, fellow pilgrims who can mentor, encourage, and counsel me in following Jesus. Amen.

For Reflection

1. What gifts and abilities has God given you? Do you feel able to use these for work of the kingdom?

2. Have you ever sensed a specific call from God to a particular type of job—or have you been able to make career choices on the basis of gospel values? What role do Christian friends play in your career direction?

3. How does doubt affect your relationship with God? What questions do you find most persistent or unsettling? Do you find doubt helpful or destructive? What resources strengthen you in times of doubt?

4. What effective ways have you found to immerse yourself in Scripture? What barriers or struggles have you faced in Bible study? Have you learned any disciplines that have helped you be consistent in reading the Scriptures?

5. Do you have a spiritual mentor or "soul friend"? If so, how has that person been helpful?

Turn the World Upside Down

Thursday, May 23: Strood to Bearsted (10 miles)
Fellow pilgrim: Arfon Jones

*For many centuries the Christian church in the West
has been closely allied with government • The way of Jesus
sometimes requires us to resist such alliance • Nationalism
can be positive if it respects the interests of all peoples
and nations • God delights in the cultural and linguistic
diversity of the world • To be strong in the face of pressure
from government or society, we need deep spiritual wells.*

A God with a Sense of Humor

My room on Watling Street was on the noisy side of the house, and rumbling vehicles disturbed my sleep during the night. Breakfast was in a greenhouse addition overlooking the garden—a lovely setting ruined by the incessant chatter of a television in the adjacent room.

However, my hosts served a wonderful "full English breakfast," prompting me to offer a playful British morning prayer: *For bacon, beans, and toast, / Praise Father, Son, and Holy Ghost.* I was grateful that God has a sense of humor even when I don't.

Meeting Arfon Jones[1] at the Rochester train station cheered me up immediately. Arfon was committed enough to the pilgrimage to take a day off from his work as General Secretary of the Evan-

My walking day usually started with a full English breakfast: eggs, sausage, baked beans, mushrooms, tomatoes, toast, various kinds of jam, juice, and coffee.

Arfon and I stopped to pray in the crypt of Rochester Cathedral.

gelical Alliance in Wales. He even got out of bed at 4:00 a.m. for an early low-fare train from Caerdydd (Cardiff) to London, and then on to Rochester.

Arfon and I paused on a busy shopping street to buy lunch supplies. Then we made our way to Rochester Cathedral and down into the basement crypt. In the bowels of that great building, we sat in silence, faintly aware of distant footsteps and buses in the urban bustle outside.

We thanked God for pilgrims who had walked the way of discipleship before us, and prayed that we would know Christ that day. Then we read a passage from the Gospel of Luke. Religious leaders of Jerusalem tried to trap Jesus in public with a question:

> *"Is it lawful for us to pay taxes to the emperor, or not?" But he perceived their craftiness and said to them, "Show me a denarius.*

Whose head and whose title does it bear?" They said, "The em-
peror's." He said to them, "Then give to the emperor the things
that are the emperor's, and to God the things that are God's."
And they were not able in the presence of the people to trap him
by what he said; and being amazed by his answer, they became
silent. (Luke 20:20-26)

If Jesus had said, "No, don't pay taxes," then his opponents could have reported his sedition to the Roman authorities. On the other hand, if he had said, "Yes, pay your taxes," then Jewish nationalists who wanted to throw off the Roman overlords could have dismissed him or tried to destroy him as a lackey of the foreign oppressors.

Instead, Jesus gave an answer that required listeners to make their own decision: "Give to the emperor the things that are the emperor's, and to God the things that are God's." Coins bore the emperor's image, and Jesus was ready to give those back to the emperor. Humans are made in the image of God, however, and every part of us belongs to God.

A Wheel of Fortune

Upstairs in the cathedral nave, Arfon and I were intrigued to find a thirteenth-century wall painting of the Wheel of Fortune. It depicts Fate turning a giant vertical wheel. On the left side two characters ride toward the top, where a third person—perhaps a king—sits perched above everyone else. The right side of the painting has been destroyed, but must have portrayed other unfortunate persons with declining fortune. The man at the top is just about to lose his position and swing around to the bottom.

The painting reminded medieval pilgrims that positions of political, social, or economic power are precarious and often momentary.

Discipleship and political power was our topic for the day. We

**Thirteenth-century wall painting of Fate turning the Wheel of
Fortune at Rochester Cathedral**

found a vivid reminder of both when we stepped out of the cathedral. Directly in front of us stood the ruins of an impressive castle, where kings and nobles once sought security behind thick walls and crossbows.

What struck us was the close coupling of cathedral and castle. It was a visual reminder of how, over many centuries, the Christian church in England and most of Europe tied itself tightly to military might. Could Jesus ever have imagined that his followers would rely on castles and state-of-the-art weaponry to overcome their enemies?

Nationalism and the Tower of Babel

On our walk toward the edge of Rochester city, I began to probe Arfon's understanding of Christian faith and nationalism. I confessed that I have a fairly negative view of nationalism, since it sometimes expresses itself as a morally blind determination to support "my country, right or wrong."

Some Christians in America (and elsewhere) seem to confuse loyalty to nation with loyalty to God. They even go so far as to say it is a Christian duty to support whatever policies governments contrive. The very word *nationalism* makes me uncomfortable because I associate it with flag-waving patriotism that shades over into idolatry.

Arfon listened carefully as I described what I had seen of nationalism in the most powerful nation on earth. Then he began to explain what nationalism means to someone from a politically powerless, small country like Wales. The history of Wales is long and complex, but the basic observation Arfon made was that for centuries England has controlled Wales and for a long time tried to destroy Welsh language and culture.

In 1536 Wales ceased to exist as a separate nation. Against the will of most Welsh people, it became part of the realm of England. The 1536 Act of Union, issued by the king of England, noted that the people of Wales "do daily use a speche nothing like ne [nor] consonaunt to the naturall mother tonge used within this Realme [of England]," and stated that England would do its best "utterly to extirpe all and singuler the senister usages and customs differing from the same."

The king of England declared that, whether they liked it or not, the people of Wales would be "for ever fromhensforthe united and annexed to and with his Realme of Englande."

In the nineteenth century the English enforced a "Welsh Not" policy in the school system of Wales. Matthew Arnold, an influential English educationalist, wrote in 1855, "It must always be the desire of a government to render its dominions, as far as possible, homogeneous. . . . Sooner or later the difference of language between Wales and England will probably be effaced, . . . an event which is socially and politically so desirable."

School children caught speaking Welsh had to wear a sign around their necks that said "Welsh Not." They wore that until they caught other students speaking Welsh and reported them to the teacher.

The Welsh language is precious to Arfon. He explained his reasons for that by citing the Tower of Babel story in Genesis 11. In that account, early humanity shared one language and one culture, which they exploited in trying to consolidate power:

Then they said, "Come, let us build ourselves a city, and a tower with its top in the heavens, and let us make a name for ourselves; otherwise we shall be scattered abroad upon the face of the whole earth." The Lord came down to see the city and the tower, which mortals had built. And the Lord said, "Look, they are one people, and they have all one language; and this is only the beginning of what they will do; nothing that they propose to do will now be impossible for them. Come, let us go down, and confuse their language there, so that they will not understand one another's speech." So the Lord scattered them abroad from there over the face of all the earth, and they left off building the city. Therefore it was called Babel, because there the Lord confused the language of all the earth; and from there the Lord scattered them abroad over the face of all the earth. (Genesis 11:1-9)

Arfon expounded on the passage:

People often use that story to argue that the diversity of languages is a curse on humanity and a hindrance to world peace. But that is a misunderstanding of what happened. Humankind set out to build a city and a tower "with its top in the heavens." They did this so they would not be "scattered abroad upon the face of the whole earth." Humanity was acting against God's command in Genesis 1:28 to "fill the earth" (Genesis 1:28). So God acted to "confuse their language" and scatter people again across the world—which was his intention from the beginning!

What happened at Babel was God's judgment on the human attempt to create a single (but rebellious) culture. Sinful humans wanted to rule their own life and destiny. They wanted to be in control, and did not want to be diverse and vulnerable. God wanted human culture to be varied, with people basing relationships on faith in God rather than in themselves or their political organization.

Taken into Custody

Arfon and I reached the south edge of Rochester and looked out over the gently rolling meadows and fields of county Kent. On the crest of a hill where we stood was perched an ominous-looking complex of buildings with a sign that read, "H M [Her Majesty's] Prison." We skirted around the place on a quiet road.

Arfon commented that several times he had served a prison sentence for nonviolent civil disobedience. This was related to his part in campaigns to promote the use and preservation of the

Welsh language. When he was a youth, the English government still refused to put bilingual road signs on highways in Wales, and there was no Welsh language television channel.

On one occasion Arfon, with other members of the Welsh Language Society, decided to break into a television transmitting station, scramble files, and destroy a token piece of equipment. Since Arfon had already been convicted of destroying English-only road signs, he received a six-month prison sentence.

With my intention of taking pictures throughout the Pilgrim walk, I asked Arfon if I could photograph him in front of the prison. He obligingly stood near the barbed-wire perimeter fence while I focused my camera. Then we stopped by the front entrance, where I snapped a few more frames.

We were no more than a hundred yards past the prison when two guards came briskly down the road behind us. "Can we speak with you please?" one of them said with a no-nonsense tone of authority. "Did you take pictures here? This is government property and you are not permitted to take photographs. Come with us."

I should have known! There is fear in Britain about terrorist attacks, and on half a dozen occasions, we actually heard bombs go off in London during our five years there. On our way to the prison with the guards, I remembered reading that certain government buildings may not be photographed. Terrorists might use the pictures to plan an attack or a prison escape.

The guards took us into the "Visitors Centre," a small office complex and guardhouse just outside the main gate. "Who are you, and why are you taking pictures?" an earnest officer inquired.

We gave our names. "I'm a Christian," I said, "and I'm walking the Pilgrims' Way to Canterbury. Arfon is walking with me today. We're reading the Bible and talking and praying as we go. I expect to do some writing about the journey, and I'm taking pictures along the way."

Arfon Jones in front of a barbed-wire fence at the prison near Rochester

All the while, I was silently praying that the guards would not confiscate my film. The officer squinted one eye and asked for identification. He disappeared with our papers into a back room, while another guard made polite conversation with us.

A few minutes later the officer reappeared. "I'm going to let you go," he said briskly, "and I hope you have a good walk to Canterbury. Don't take any more pictures of government buildings."

We agreed, and I gently let out a sigh of relief.

"Oh, before you go," he continued, "we're going to run a computer check to make sure you don't have a criminal record."

"I must tell you, I do have a criminal record," Arfon volunteered respectfully.

"For what?" the officer asked.

Arfon briefly explained the circumstances, and the computer check revealed nothing more sinister. Soon we were on our way down a steep hillside to a footbridge across the busy M2 motorway. A closed-circuit camera kept an unblinking eye on us from a tall pole at one end of the footbridge.

I commented to Arfon that he did not act frightened by the prison guards and treated them with respect.

He responded,

I have been in prison many times for the Welsh language campaign. Prison officers often try to show their authority. When you arrive as a new prisoner, they strip you naked, search you, and try to intimidate you. I always tried to show them respect and let them sense something of the love of Jesus. I hope the way we responded to the officers today will be a witness to the gospel.

Did you notice that at the end the officer said, "I hope your pilgrimage goes well"? Who knows? He may be on some kind of pilgrimage himself. You and I may be just one link in a chain of witnesses to show him the love of Jesus.

Sometimes, Arfon said, we have opportunity to speak specifics of the gospel when we witness to others.

We can talk about Jesus and his teaching and explain the cross and the resurrection. Often that's not possible, though, and it's never right to force the gospel on anyone. But that prison officer knows we are Christians. He watched how we behaved—and he might have a friend elsewhere who is a believer, whom God will use to show him more of the love of Jesus.

A Christian Involved in Politics

The Welsh Language Society—which organized the campaigns Arfon joined as a young man—is not a Christian organization. Arfon and other committed believers, though, had a leavening influence within the movement.

"In the early years of my involvement in the Society, there was a lot of talk about turning to violence, about taking a Marxist and potentially violent approach to change," he said. "As followers of Jesus, my fellow Christians and I had to go about our protest in a different way."

Arfon is a modest man and would never inflate his own role in any achievement. It was clear to me, though, that his voice had helped turn the Welsh Language Society into an effective, self-consciously nonviolent agent of change. The Society ended up adopting a strategy of "no violence of fist, mouth, or heart." I could see by Arfon's demeanor, when we were apprehended that morning, that he puts such an approach of love into practice.

I asked Arfon the familiar question of what he would do if a violent person were attacking someone he loved.

I don't think it's ever right for me to respond with violence. If someone broke into my house, I'd try to protect my wife. But I wouldn't kill that person. I am very aware that there's a lot of potential for violence within me, but I would never claim that it is good or right. Under the grace of God, I have to deal with that. In the likeness of Christ, I have to resist the temptation to express violence—even though I will express indignation at an injustice.

How do followers of Jesus come to such a measured level of response and conviction? Arfon reflected,

Long before a situation of violence arises, we must develop disciplines of prayer, Bible reading, community, and accountability. How we deal with finances is especially important. If we live on our individual finances and have our faith in things, then our relationship with God is just a hobby. But if we become generous givers, *hilarious* givers [from the Greek word *hilaros*, "cheerful," in 2 Corinthians 9:7], then we're constantly in a situation of dependence on God. We need the faith community, and the community needs us. Then we say with Paul, "I can do all things through him who strengthens me" [Philippians 4:13].

I was intrigued by Arfon drawing a close connection between our attitude toward financial matters and our tendency to be violent. If we hold tightly to material things, he said, we probably will use whatever means possible to defend them.

We stopped on the footpath. Arfon picked up a stick to draw a line in the dirt, and waved the tip of the stick back and forth across it. "People often think of becoming a Christian as crossing a borderline into a new place," he said. "In fact, it's much more a matter of turning around on a line and going the opposite way—toward God instead of away from God."

The tip of Arfon's stick followed along the line he had drawn, then reversed direction. The way of the world is to head one direction toward power, self-sufficiency, and violence. The way of Jesus is to go the other direction toward God, finding security and *shalom* in the community of those who live by gospel values.

The Kingdom of God Embraces the World

I pressed Arfon to say more about his understanding of the relationship between the way of Jesus and the way of the world.

The kingdom of God is not an *alternative* to the kingdoms of the world. Rather, the kingdom of God *embraces* the world. The fact that you've paid for your camera, Nelson, means you are part of the economic order of wider society. You are political; you are part of "the system." Jesus said, "Give to the emperor the things that are the emperor's, and to God the things that are God's." This is not a dualism, not a way of dividing life into two separate spheres. Paying taxes to Caesar should be something we do *within* our loyalty to God.

But what if governments act in ways that are contrary to the example and teaching of Jesus? Arfon responded,

In that case, God always comes first. When early followers of Jesus were arrested and put on trial, they said, "We must obey God rather than any human authority" [Acts 5:29]. Paul says rulers "are not a terror to good conduct, but to bad," and government is "God's servant for your good" [Romans 13:3-4]. I am not an anarchist, but I am for careful discernment.

Turning the World Upside Down

I recalled the accusations brought against first-century Christians at Thessalonica, including a man named Jason. A band of ruffians gathered a mob to drag the Christians before the city authorities and accuse them as follows:

"These people who have been turning the world upside down have come here also, and Jason has entertained them as guests. They are all acting contrary to the decrees of the emperor, saying that there is another king named Jesus." The people and the city officials were disturbed when they heard this, and after they had taken bail from Jason and the others, they let them go.
(Acts 17:6, 7)

A radical commitment to the way of Jesus sometimes looks to others like turning the world upside down. Loving enemies, caring for the weak, sharing possessions, and refusing to take revenge—these all seem anarchistic or threatening to people conditioned by conventional politics. Arfon continued:

When rulers don't act in ways God intended governments
to act, then we should respond like Shadrach, Meshach, and
Abednego, the Jewish lads who refused to bow down and
worship a golden statue when King Nebuchadnezzar of
Babylon ordered them to do so [Daniel 3]. Our response to
government and to authority must always be in light of
whether or not governments are being obedient to God's
calling for them, and whether or not we would be obedient
to Christ if we did what governments said. It is possible for
government itself to become a source of evil, and then
Christians should refuse to cooperate.

This talk of selective disobedience to government seemed
paradoxical, coming from a man who calls himself a "Welsh nationalist." How could Arfon use such language when nationalism is often an excuse for putting country first, even above loyalty to God?

He gave a good account of his position:

Just because sex and money are misused doesn't make them
evil. The same is true with nationalism. I believe God intends for people groups within the human family to express
a "polycentric nationalism." All peoples can celebrate their
own culture and history, while respecting the rights and
needs of other peoples. To be a polycentric nationalist
means you must be nonviolent.

When violence creeps into the situation, you are violat-
ing some other nation or some other group. I'm not so interested in supporting and maintaining a particular government. But I think it is part of God's love for creation that he
wants to protect the rich diversity of language, culture, literature, music, and art.

Wealth and Care for Our World

Another walker met us as we talked, coming the opposite way with two enormous Great Danes and a tiny hairless Chinese dog. We stopped to visit briefly. Out of curiosity, I inquired what it costs to feed such animals.

"About £10 [$16] per week for the big dogs," the owner replied. "And one of them just had a £600 [$960] leg operation." A few minutes later, with the dogs and their owner well behind us, Arfon commented that it costs more to feed a cat in the United Kingdom than is usually spent to feed a child in some countries of the world. Our conversation shifted to a broader reflection on when and how Christians should become involved in matters of local or international justice.

Arfon explained that his commitment to justice included a deep desire to care for the physical earth. His wife, Rachel, works for an environmental organization called Friends of the Earth. He noted that one acre of rain forest in the tropics has more species of life in it than all of the United Kingdom. Christians have an obligation to care for the environment in both places.

Some of our Christian friends think it's inappropriate to work for Friends of the Earth because Buddhists and people from other world religions are involved. But people who raise questions about such involvement may themselves be allied with business interests that are destroying the earth. Many Christians are too concerned about getting their doctrine right. God is above that; he cares about relationships and justice.

If Christians hadn't gotten involved in the Welsh nationalist movement, the Marxists would have taken it down a more violent path. It is possible to get into a political or economic situation and address urgent issues from a Christian perspective. If we don't do that, then less-creative or even violent ways will prevail.

Just after noon we passed Robin Hood Pub, and approached the village of Kit's Coty. Our path followed along a busy highway, then descended downhill through a sunken path canopied with branches. It opened out to one of Britain's many prehistoric stone monuments. Called by moderns the Kit's Coty House Burial Chamber, it consists today of three massive vertical stones capped by a fourth in a horizontal position. These few remaining stones once were part of a neolithic "long barrow" burial chamber that measured 180 feet in length, built about 2000 B.C.

We sat on grass next to the great monument and pulled sandwiches from our rucksacks. The Welsh prayer Arfon offered was unintelligible to my ears, but not to my heart. Several times amid the clusters of consonants and full-throated syllables, I heard my own name and knew Arfon was asking God to bless me as well as the food.

Spiritual Wells to Sustain an Activist

Back on the road again, I asked Arfon what spiritual wells have kept him from running dry during his many years of church work and political engagement. Almost reflexively, he pointed to the Bible. "Once when I was in prison, I was locked up for twenty-three hours a day. In two weeks, I read the entire Bible once and the New Testament twice. I just read it like you would read a novel."

Too often, he said, people only read the Bible in short segments—and never feel the cadence of great literature. "Sometime try reading, say, Jeremiah straight from beginning to end," he suggested. "You get a new sense of intimacy with the author and the message."

Arfon's ongoing love of Scripture has motivated him to set aside ninety minutes daily before breakfast to help with revision of a modern Welsh translation of the Bible. The translation was published in 1988, but some Welsh readers think it needs refine-

Arfon Jones stops for lunch at the prehistoric Kit's Coty stone monument.

ment and further scholarship.

I asked Arfon what some of his favorite Bible passages are. "I have trouble quoting them in English." He laughed and gave an English version of Zechariah 4:6: "Not by might, nor by power, but by my spirit, says the Lord of hosts." It's a good verse for Christian peacemakers, he noted, because it reminds us that political and social change will happen by God's power and not just by our efforts.

"On a personal level, change also comes by God's Spirit," Arfon continued. He quoted Colossians 3:13-14: "Bear with one another and, if anyone has a complaint against another, forgive each other; just as the Lord has forgiven you, so you also must forgive. Above all, clothe yourselves with love."

Too often, Arfon said, Christians are good at saying, "God has forgiven me," but are not so good at forgiving others. "I have a severe temper at times," Arfon confessed. "It's a battle to keep it under control. I fail so often. If it's a person that angers me, I ask God to help me look at the person and see Jesus in them. We need not only to *reflect* Jesus, but to *see* Jesus in others. Often that's the hardest with people closest to you."

A discernible look of pain crossed Arfon's face. He recounted a time fifteen years ago when he didn't care for himself in body and spirit.

In the 1970s I had grand mal epilepsy. In 1977 I was healed of that illness. But two years later, my mother died of an epileptic seizure. I couldn't escape the question: Why did God heal me of epilepsy when my mother died of it? I determined that since God allowed me to live, I would give myself wholly to God's service.

At that time I was National Youth Officer for my denomination and worked extremely hard. Friends said I should slow down, but I didn't. I took one week of holiday in six years. I didn't take proper Sabbath rest. Eventually I suffered total exhaustion and had to be off work for twenty months.

During that difficult time, Arfon drew deeply from wells of prayer and Scripture. Many of the psalms, he discovered, really "go to the depths" of suffering. They provide a voice of prayer for someone who feels alone and devastated.

In late afternoon Arfon and I trudged down off the North Downs hills, across a vast field of rape oil plant in fluorescent yellow flower, and to the train station at Bearsted village. As Arfon's train throttled up to leave the station, I reflected on how grateful I was for such a passionate and committed friend. Weary and hungry, I extracted from my pocket a hand-drawn map of Bearsted that would take me to the home of an elderly widow— my hostess for the night.

Prayer

Thank you, Creator, for the wonderful diversity of peoples and cultures in the world. Thank you for the government and institutions of society in the country where I live. Help me to be discerning, to support government and social institutions when they serve humanity, and to withhold support or to resist when they abuse power. Open my eyes to see the relationship between patterns of living in my country and needs of the world elsewhere. Make me a citizen of your kingdom first, and let all other loyalties be subordinate to my allegiance to Jesus. Amen.

For Reflection

1. What does nationalism mean in your experience? Can you think of examples of healthy and unhealthy nationalism from modern history or current events?

2. How do you feel about Arfon's approach of nonviolent resistance and civil disobedience in the face of unjust government policy? How does his approach compare with the conflicts Jesus and the early Christians had with authorities?

3. Where would you "draw the line" in how far you would go to obey government? What might a government expect you to do that you could not do because you are a Christian?

4. Do you think of the kingdom of God as part of the world or separate from it? How might your answer to that question affect your involvement in society?

5. In what ways could you become more involved in care for the environment and in working for justice for people in poor parts of the world?

6. In what ways do you care for your own physical and emotional well-being?

8

Risk Everything for God

Friday, May 24: Bearsted to Charing (10 miles)
Fellow pilgrims: Alan and Eleanor Kreider

We need refreshment and nurture in regular prayer and worship •
Spiritual growth usually happens in small steps rather than great
leaps • God is present even in experiences of suffering to restore life
and hope • Communion reminds us that, in Jesus, God himself
suffered • God was willing to absorb the pain caused by human sin
• We know God most fully in risking everything to follow Jesus •
God may call us to a place of seeming inadequacy, where we have to
trust in him • Prayer can be enriched by attention to sound, sight,
touch, and posture • We need to tell the stories of God's faithfulness.

A Boisterous Morning Greeting

At 6:30 a.m. the door of my bedroom burst open, and in
bounded a great Black Labrador! It was Penny, friendly pet of Inez
Kingston, my gracious hostess at Bearsted village. Inez, a widow
in her midsixties, had generously given me her own bed on the
ground floor while she slept upstairs.

The dog apparently was accustomed to giving her a boister-
ous morning greeting. Pleased to offer me the wake-up call, Penny's tail thumped eagerly against the side of a dresser. Her embarrassed owner soon was at the door, full of apologies.

It would have taken a lot to diminish my opinion of Inez and

Sid in front of the Wesleyan Chapel in Bearsted

her hospitality. The previous evening she had invited two friends from her local (Wesleyan) church, Sid and Olive, to join us at the dinner table. Despite my aching muscles, I savored both the excellent meal and the table fellowship.

Recently Inez had moved into her modest house. She was adjusting to living alone after her husband's death. At the suggestion of a mutual acquaintance, she had agreed to host me overnight during her last week of work before retirement. She is a friend to many, and others pay back in kind: a bulletin board in the kitchen was filled with housewarming cards. She also prays. Fastened to her bedroom dresser was a note: "Long-standing problem? Try kneeling."

Inez left for work in the morning before I finished breakfast. Over dinner the night before, Sid offered to show me the chapel by the train station where he, Olive, and Inez worship. At the appointed hour after breakfast, I met him there, and he showed me around the humble building.

"We struggle a bit as a congregation," Sid said seriously after the tour. "We're an elderly group, and there aren't enough young families." Sid himself is well into retirement. "Some of us who *are* a bit younger do some mission in the community. Our minister is very busy, since he also has five other churches to look after."

We went to the front of the little chapel and stood by the altar. I prayed, thanking God for Sid and Olive's years of commitment to the mission of the church. I asked God to take their offering of faithfulness and service, and use it as seeds for the kingdom that would bear fruit in ways they could not even imagine. Sid seemed moved by the prayer, and his voice caught as he in turn read a beautiful Pentecost prayer.

Needing a Sabbath Rest

My fellow pilgrims for the day, Alan and Eleanor Kreider, were not on the 10:18 a.m. train to Bearsted as I expected. The station manager had a message saying they would arrive at eleven o'clock. I was glad for a bit of silence and solitude at the tiny station.

This was the beginning of my second week on the road. A cumulative physical and emotional weariness settled into my bones. In astonishment I thought, *Why hadn't I planned a Sabbath rest into my pilgrim walk? Why did I think it would be a good idea to press hard, talking and walking and writing for twelve days nonstop?* At the planning stage, the whole idea of being outdoors for twelve days sounded like such a welcome relief from the telephone, computer, and doorbell that it didn't even occur to me that I might become exhausted!

I felt chastened by my weariness, especially in view of Arfon's story the day before about working to exhaustion himself. I tend to take projects and assignments seriously, even to the point of working beyond what is healthy. I want to grow spiritually and emotionally so I'm able to work hard and then rest.

God could have put a consumer label on each person: "Please follow instructions. Manufacturer not responsible for misuse." The instructions for a Sabbath are clear in the Bible: Keep one day out of seven "holy" (set apart) for rest and worship:

> *Six days you shall labor and do all your work. But the seventh day is a sabbath to the Lord your God; you shall not do any work. . . . For in six days the Lord made heaven and earth, the sea, and all that is in them,* but rested the seventh day.
> (Exodus 20:8-11)

I used to think the Sabbath was a special day for God. I've come to see it as a gift from God for human emotional and spiritual well-being. We need rest for our bodies and time to renew our souls in worship and recreation. Jesus was not legalistic about observing the Sabbath, but the Gospels portray him making time for solitude, rest, and prayer.

On one occasion the disciples were exhausted from a preaching and healing tour that was so frenetic they didn't even have time to eat. Jesus told them to take some rest. The weary followers "went away in the boat to a deserted place by themselves" (Mark 6:32). I love that verse, perhaps because I love sailing and have found that a few hours on the water can restore my soul.

Wind and Rain

As foretold by the station manager, Alan and Eleanor Kreider stepped off the eleven o'clock train. We set out on a country road toward the hills a mile away. Aside from my wife, Ellen, and daughters, no other pilgrims on my walk had known me so long or so well. Eleanor is my wife's aunt, and Alan was a favorite history professor of mine twenty years ago at Goshen College in Indiana.

Eleanor and Alan Kreider at the village church in Thurnham

Alan and Eleanor are mission workers with Mennonite Board of Missions. Both teach part-time at Regent's Park College in Oxford. They also speak and preach widely on discipleship issues. They laughed as I told them the story of Arfon and me being taken into prison. "The place was like a great sleeping lion," Eleanor said, "and you tweaked its tail!"

We stopped at the tiny village of Thurnham, at the bottom of the North Downs hills, to read the Bible and pray inside a lovely old church. It started to rain when we emerged. "Well, the British say Americans want a shower every morning!" Eleanor said.

It was cold and wet, and the idea of a hot shower in the bathroom sounded better than what faced us on the hilltops ahead. Brisk winds and cold, driving rain assailed us at the top of the ridge. Waterproof jackets helped, but we still got soaked from head to toe on the right (windward) side. My endless scrawling into a small notepad had to cease in the open fields. But when we got to a tree or any kind of shelter from the rain, I pulled out my pad and made a quick record of the conversation.

Three Kinds of Pilgrimage

Eleanor remembered meeting walkers on the great slopes of Switzerland:

> Experienced long-distance mountain walkers go very slowly. They plod on, one small step after another—and laugh at the tourists who go fast and then fall over! Perhaps that's one way to think of Christian discipleship—one small step after another.

Sometimes I'm tempted to compare myself with spiritual giants, men and women who have climbed great mountains of hardship or suffering in obedience to God. In comparison to their faithfulness, I feel like a spiritual pygmy. Eleanor's image of discipleship as one step after another was a good reminder that spiritual growth often happens in small and undramatic ways. Healthy growth happens when we keep our focus on where God wants us to be, not on the performance of others.

The topic of walking generated discussion of different types of pilgrimage, and together we thought of three:

> 1. *A wandering pilgrimage.* An example of this would be the anonymous nineteenth-century author of a spiritual classic known as *The Way of a Pilgrim.* The writer spent many years wandering across Russia and Siberia on a quest to know God.
> 2. *A round-trip pilgrimage to a significant place.* For centuries pilgrims across Europe trekked to Santiago de Compostela in Spain, doing penance for sins or seeking healing. Back home again, their lives were different because they had made the journey.

3. *A huge journey, with a promised but still unknown destination, from which it is unlikely one will ever return.* Abraham and Sarah, called to leave the land of their forebears in Mesopotamia for a distant promised land, would be examples of this (Genesis 12).

Christian discipleship, we decided, is most like the third type of pilgrimage. Alan said,

> It is a collective walk, though. Christians are a pilgrim *people,* and we follow the guidebook of someone who has gone before. What God said to Abraham and Sarah, Jesus says to us: Go to a place I will show you. We don't have a map, we don't know exactly what the journey will hold, and there will be orienteering at every step of the journey.

Bread and Cup as Symbols of Discipleship

"That's the risk of discipleship," Eleanor observed. "We don't know at every step that we're getting it right. We don't know what the provision will be at the next stop. But we are called to be 'eucharistic' (thankful) that there is provision for our needs."

Hearing Eleanor talk of thankfulness and God's provision reminded me of the enormous suffering she endured as a young woman, when her first husband and their daughter, Joy, both died of cancer within a short period of time. How could anyone survive such trauma and emerge with the deep joy that is so evident in Eleanor's life?

She told me once that there is never a day, even decades later, that she does not somehow grieve for her child. Such enormous sorrow could become a heavy chain of despair or self-pity. But a miracle of God's grace has happened in Eleanor's life, transforming even a grief so great into a reservoir of mercy, hope, and sensitivity to others. No one would ever convince Eleanor that suf-

Eleanor Kreider, soaked by rain on the open hillsides

fering of that kind is good. But she is living evidence that from the deepest reaches of spiritual and emotional death, God can raise abundant life.

Death and resurrection are at the center of Christian faith, and Eleanor has spent years studying and writing on the meaning of the bread and cup in Christian community and discipleship. (She is author of the book *Communion Shapes Character.*) At our time of prayer and Scripture reading at the church in Thurnham, Alan, Eleanor, and I had read an account of Jesus' last meal with his disciples before he died:

> *Then [Jesus] took a cup, and after giving thanks he said, "Take this and divide it among yourselves; for I tell you that from now on I will not drink of the fruit of the vine until the kingdom of God comes." Then he took a loaf of bread, and when he had given thanks, he broke it and gave it to them, saying, "This is my*

*body, which is given for you. Do this in remembrance of me."
And he did the same with the cup after supper, saying, "This cup
that is poured out for you is the new covenant in my blood."*

(Luke 22:14-23)

Eleanor explained how symbols of the Eucharist help us understand God's provision for his people through the community:

When Jesus gave the bread to his disciples, he said, "Take this and share it among you." He didn't give bread directly to each disciple. Taking the bread and cup is not a private or individualistic experience. It happens in the context of a community of believers who intend to share not only the Lord's Table, but also the material and spiritual substance of their lives.

There is a story from Mark's Gospel about the disciples James and John asking for prominent positions of power in the coming kingdom of God:

*"Grant us to sit, one at your right hand and one at your left, in
your glory." But Jesus said to them, "You do not know what you
are asking. Are you able to drink the cup that I drink, or be baptized with the baptism that I am baptized with?" They replied,
"We are able." Then Jesus said to them, "The cup that I drink
you will drink; and with the baptism with which I am baptized,
you will be baptized; but to sit at my right hand or at my left is
not mine to grant, but it is for those for whom it has been prepared." (Mark 10:37-40)*

Eleanor used this incident to add a layer of meaning to Christian communion:

Jesus here is talking about the cup of discipleship. Are we able to drink it? The cup is Jesus' life poured out for us, and now we are called to pour out our lives in obedience to God and service to others.

Eleanor added that she likes when communion wine actually is poured into a cup in the presence of the congregation, to symbolize the way Jesus poured out his life and calls us to do the same.

A God Who Suffered for Our Sin

On the night before he died, Jesus first spoke of bread and wine in the language now familiar at Christian communion. Jesus was about to "drink a cup" of suffering which he did not deserve. He was about to pay a penalty that many would deem appropriate for the thieves crucified with him, but not for the sinless Son of God. Alan pointed out that when Jesus prayed, "Remove this cup from me" in the Garden of Gethsemane on the eve of his death (Luke 22:42), he may have had in mind the following psalm:

> *For in the hand of the Lord there is a cup*
> *   with foaming wine, well mixed;*
> *he will pour a draught from it,*
> *   and all the wicked of the earth*
> *   shall drain it down to the dregs.* (Psalm 75:8)

"That is the cup of wrath that Jesus drank for us," Alan explained. But did Jesus take upon himself a punishment that God his Father meted out? Couldn't God have worked out some more charitable arrangement than to put his Son through such an ordeal? Couldn't God, for example, simply have chosen to forgive the sins of the world without making anybody suffer like Jesus did on the cross?

It would not be in the character of God to "get even." But the world functions in such a way that selfish, violent, or sinful behavior usually ends up causing someone to suffer. Evil generates

its own whirlwind of destruction, misery, and death. Yet the Hebrew prophets knew that God was able to direct even the evil
acts of sinful people toward fulfillment of his divine plan. (For example, Isaiah 45:1-7 tells how God used "his anointed," the pagan
king Cyrus, to liberate the Jewish exiles when Cyrus conquered
Babylon.)

God does not design or call forth evil, but neither does he
routinely intervene to neutralize the awful effects of evil. Some-
body, somewhere, ends up suffering for human sin. When Jesus
died on the cross, he was willing to absorb the suffering caused
by people who felt threatened by his message of forgiveness and
hope. God held a "cup with foaming wine," the measure of suffering that happens when humans sin—and Jesus drank that cup.

Here the nature of God becomes most complex. We see God
in *both* Father and Son. God, who is able to turn even the bale-
ful effects of evil toward some good, chose to turn the suffering
caused by sin onto himself in the person of Jesus the Son. God
absorbed torture and death, the worst that human malice can
produce, and then raised Jesus to life again. Jesus' death on a
cross shows the magnitude of God's love for the world. Jesus' resurrection shows that God's power to redeem is far greater than
even the most dire circumstances.

With the death and resurrection of Jesus playing so central a
role in Christian understanding of God, it's not surprising that
communion becomes a focal point of worship, discipleship, and
fellowship among believers. My own (Anabaptist) tradition says
there is nothing extraordinary about communion bread and wine
in and of themselves. There is no physical change in this food
when a worship leader blesses the Lord's table. But there is a fundamental change in people who eat this meal together, remembering Jesus' death and giving themselves to God as Jesus did.

Communion is a foretaste of a time when the kingdom of God
will come in its fullness. At the first Lord's Supper, on the night

before he died, Jesus said, "From now on I will not drink of the fruit of the vine until the kingdom of God comes" (Luke 22:18). Paul reminded his readers that every time they eat the bread and drink the cup, they "proclaim the Lord's death until he comes" (1 Corinthians 11:26). Communion looks back to remember Jesus' suffering, and looks forward to celebrate his final victory over suffering and sin at the end of time.

An Antidote to Worry

Theological reflection and a brisk pace of walking kept us reasonably warm. Nevertheless, we were glad to come down off the hills at Hollingbourne for hot soup at a pub called "The Dirty Habit." The name of the pub seemed curious until we noticed a sign on the building that depicted a monk wearing the habit of his religious order. His garment was as muddy as our own trousers and boots!

Our afternoon conversation turned to the topic of risk-taking, and we agreed that Jesus' willingness to embrace suffering and even death was a high-risk strategy for showing love. Eleanor quoted a Christian friend from New Zealand who said, "The hardest saying of Jesus is the instruction not to worry" (Matthew 6:34).

As an antidote to worry, this friend took seriously another saying of Jesus: "Give to everyone who begs from you" (Luke 6:30). He found that the more he was willing to let go of possessions and share them with others, the less he worried about material things.

Eleanor said,

If we always plan for our own security, we don't ever see God doing surprising, hilarious, communal deeds of hope. It's our drive for security that keeps the door shut on knowing God in a deep way.

Alan added,

> If we won't take risks, we're trapped. If we say we won't take any steps of discipleship until the outcome is clear, then we're acting like insurance companies who qualify the risk of taking on a particular client and make actuarial calculations.

Taking risks in obedience to God goes beyond financial matters to include how we use our time and gifts. Alan said thoughtfully,

> I've learned that God sometimes wants us to be in a position of inadequacy. If I had just followed my gifting, I probably should have continued as a full-time university teacher.

Here I could concur, recalling how I sat in Alan's history courses as a college student in America and marveled at his ability to inspire and motivate students. Then Alan and Eleanor left for England, to uncertain and unsung roles of hospitality and teaching in the church. God moved Alan from a secure academic position, where he was more than adequate to the task, and put him in a cross-cultural situation, where he often has felt inadequate. Alan observed,

> Jesus has a way of going to problem places, and he calls us with him into situations of brokenness and confusion and conflict. In these settings we can't find our own way forward. We'll just make things worse. But God is there, waiting to give us resources of wisdom and strength and Spirit. If we're humble and trusting, we can receive God's reality, letting God make clear what the way of Jesus will be in each situation.

A Step into Insufficiency

I asked Alan what counsel he might have for other pilgrims, and he replied,

Take one step into insufficiency. Experience God's presence and strength in that moment of inadequacy, and then a new step will confront you. Once you start walking that way, momentum develops. God's grace is not necessary unless we're in a situation in which we can't live without it.

When asked for an illustration of this in his own life, Alan remembered being called upon to debate the morality of nuclear weapons in 1982, at the height of the Cold War. At a prominent church in central London, Alan debated against an air marshal and the former British chief of defence. This was the first of Alan's many public debates on Christians and war. He confessed,

I found debating tough. I was out of my area of expertise, and the other debaters were at the top of their field. In psychological terms, I'm a "feeling type," not a "thinking type" of person, and I get rattled! But in the end, it was the air marshal who got rattled. He was used to giving orders, not to debating the basics of national military policy in public.

I was eager to know what spiritual disciplines undergird the risky discipleship Alan and Eleanor have practiced for many years. They agreed that the most important was prayer. Eleanor said, "The apostle Paul tells us to 'pray without ceasing' " (1 Thessalonians 5:17). At first Alan and Eleanor were hesitant to speak much about their personal practice of prayer, but they revealed more when I persisted with questions.

Eleanor began:

There's no one form of prayer that everyone must follow.
People are different and pray in different ways. You can pray
while washing dishes! About three times a week, Alan and I
pray together. We like to use prayer books such as those
from Catholic and Anglican traditions, or from the Taizé
community. We take a liturgy from such sources, and always
use the Psalms—sometimes with a recording of sung psalms.

We always use a traditional canticle [song] such as the
"Magnificat" (Luke 1:46-55) or the "Te Deum" (composed in
Latin by the early church). We pray the Lord's Prayer, use a
collect (a short prayer from a prayer book), and then offer
free prayer with no particular structure. There are certain
people we always pray for: churches, acquaintances, specific
needs. Our prayer time always includes silence.

In Syria, Eleanor said, Christians carry prayer beads in their
pockets as a physical reminder of God. When my daughter Laura
visited Eleanor in Oxford, Eleanor gave her a simple homemade
string of varied beads. Each stone or bead could represent a particular person or topic, organizing Laura's prayer time with a tactile reminder.

"This is my daddy bead," Laura said with love in her eyes
when she came home from Oxford. She was pointing to the stone
that reminds her to pray for me. Laura is an artistic and visual
person, learning to integrate that part of herself into worship.
Some people prefer to make written lists of people and topics for
prayer. Others use photographs or music.

Alan said physical posture and surroundings affect prayer.

I like to be comfortable in body, sitting well, and relaxed. I
like to look at something beautiful. Sometimes we use the
Lord's Prayer as an outline. We read it phrase-by-phrase, letting each part be the heading for an aspect of prayer.

(See below for an example of using the Lord's Prayer in this way.)

Tell the Story

Immersing themselves in the Bible also has been an important discipline for Alan and Eleanor. "Sometimes verses will pop off the page and command our attention," they said. Their Bibles have dates and comments written in the margins, times and circumstances when a few verses were particularly meaningful. This allows them later to remember and celebrate the way they experienced God at a given time in life.

"We need to be conscious of God and to name that awareness," Alan said. He urges other followers of Jesus to keep a journal, and to have a "spiritual friend" with whom they regularly share insights and concerns.

We need to *tell* each other about the goodness of God. Different generations, if they love each other, must be in dialogue about what God has done. Jesus said, "I came that they may have life, and have it abundantly" [John 10:10]. We need to share that abundance with one another. Our discipleship and our ethics grow out of experiencing God. We act toward others as God acted toward us.

In late afternoon, Alan, Eleanor, and I came down off the hills and entered the historic Saxon village of Charing. Rising into the gloom of dusk was the thirteenth-century Church of St. Peter and St. Paul. Tradition claimed that this lovely church once housed the very block upon which John the Baptist was beheaded, brought back from the Holy Land by Richard the Lionhearted! Not taken in by that fanciful old tale, we made our way past a parade of shops and medieval houses to the train station. I bid my walking partners Godspeed and turned my aching feet toward

Medieval architecture in the village of Charing

dinner and bed at the Royal Oak Inn.

The following outline may help you use the Lord's Prayer (Matthew 6:9-13) as a structure for your own praying.

Prayer

Our Father in heaven, hallowed be your name.

(Thank God for his goodness, love, mercy, and faithfulness. Honor God with words of praise, or by sitting or kneeling in silence and being still in God's presence.)

Your kingdom come. Your will be done, on earth as it is in heaven.

(Imagine what the world will be like when people everywhere honor the Creator and live in love, justice, and truth. Pray that God's Spirit will change you so that such kingdom behavior becomes evident in you today. Pray for circumstances of violence or hatred around the world, places where you particularly yearn for God's kingdom to bring hope and healing.)

Give us this day our daily bread.

(Bring to God financial, social, or physical needs for yourself, your family, or your local community.)

And forgive us our debts, as we also have forgiven our debtors.

(Confess any sin or failure that stands between you and God. Pray that God will bring to awareness the sin in your life you do not yet recognize. Name people who have wronged you, and ask God for grace to forgive.)

And do not bring us to the time of trial, but rescue us from the evil one.

(Express fears or concerns you have about difficult circumstances that face you, such as doubt, broken relationships, illness, persecution, or painful choices.)

For the kingdom and the power and the glory are yours forever.

(Remind yourself that it is God's task to bring the kingdom. The burden and the credit for your walk of discipleship belong to God. Let cares of the day rest on him.)

Amen.

For Reflection

1. What rhythms of work, rest, play, and worship have you found useful or necessary in your daily and weekly life? What do you understand to be the purpose of a Sabbath?

2. Which of the three kinds of pilgrimage outlined in this chapter best describes your life journey? In what ways might you wish to change the kind of pilgrimage you are making?

3. What stories can you tell of people who suffered great pain or loss and experienced resurrection hope through their faith in God? Are there such experiences in your own life?

4. Has God called you to make any risky decisions in following Jesus? Do you recall times when you felt vulnerable or inadequate, and found that God supplied your needs?

5. What does communion mean to you? In what ways does that act of worship instruct and sustain you in following Jesus?

6. Are there any new ways of praying that you would like to incorporate into your daily life (posture, liturgy, music, visual or tactile reminders)?

Face Doubt and Danger

Saturday, May 25: Charing to Chilham (9 miles)
Fellow pilgrims: Ellen Kraybill, Nic and Ann Paton

Doubt is an essential element of faith development • Learning to trust God again may require us to let go of what once seemed necessary or secure • Journaling is a useful way to reflect on spiritual growth • The Bible has many examples of faith heroes wrestling with themselves and with God • We need spiritual companionship as we struggle with hard questions or difficult life experiences.

Three Walking Companions

Three fellow pilgrims met me at Charing for the walk to Chilham: my wife Ellen (back after a week of work as a physiotherapist in London), and our South African friends Nic and Ann Paton.

Ann was an educator and television producer in South Africa. Now she works in London as a producer for an international television news agency. Nic is a gifted musician, songwriter, and Bible College graduate. In London, he has been in transition, training for a new career in computers and asking painful questions about his relationship with God and the church.

After rain the previous day, we rejoiced in God's gift of sunshine. As a threesome, we slipped out of the village, passing the ruins of a fourteenth-century archbishop's palace. The Great Hall of the ancient complex, where kings once feasted, now serves as

Ellen with Ann and Nic Paton, near Charing village

a barn. We paused briefly to ponder the shifting tides of history, then followed the path as it cut diagonally across a grainfield.

Instead of looking down into a valley from a lofty lookout (as I had done daily during the previous week), we now were off the hilltops and into gently undulating farmland, meadows, and orchards. The landscape seemed appropriate for reflections on what it means to be "off the mountaintop" of euphoric faith and into tilled fields and working orchards of ordinary life.

The Day the World Collapsed

I wonder how Jesus' disciples felt on the day after his crucifixion. At considerable personal risk, they had followed Jesus up and down Palestine for more than two years, leaving jobs and families and security because Jesus spoke words of hope.

They had stood beside Jesus in public when he confronted powerful religious leaders, and when he made friends with tax collectors, lepers, prostitutes and other undesirables. They had witnessed blind people receive their sight, invalids spring to their feet, and sick people made well. A steady diet of teaching on the kingdom of God had filled them with confidence that a new society of justice and peace was about to appear—and then on one awful Friday, their world collapsed.

Saturday must have been hell for the disciples. Jesus had not merely died; he had been *executed* as a criminal, strung up naked to die in the sun, for all the world to see and despise.

What do you do with your life when you risk everything for God and it all ends in spectacular failure? What do you say to family and friends who perhaps thought from the start that the whole Jesus business was fanaticism and delusion? Such questions must have been on the disciples' minds when the resurrected Jesus suddenly appeared to them on Sunday evening:

While they were talking about [reports that Jesus was alive], Jesus himself stood among them and said to them, "Peace be with you." They were startled and terrified, and thought that they were seeing a ghost. He said to them, "Why are you frightened, and why do doubts arise in your hearts? Look at my hands and my feet; see that it is I myself. Touch me and see; for a ghost does not have flesh and bones as you see that I have." And when he had said this, he showed them his hands and his feet. While in their joy they were disbelieving and still wondering, he said to them, "Have you anything here to eat?" They gave him a piece of broiled fish, and he took it and ate in their presence.

(Luke 24:36-43)

There is something almost comical about the startled and disbelieving disciples feeding broiled fish to Jesus, as if to prove he was not a phantom. But they had just come through a wrenching week of spiritual disillusionment. Their keenest hopes for Israel were shattered. Now they hardly dared to hope or believe.

Questioning and Reappraisal

I have seen new believers embrace Christian faith with exuberance, with energy and joy splashing over the top to startle or even annoy friends and neighbors. A few months or years later, those same believers may be at a difficult place of uncertainty or confusion. In the flush of newfound faith in Jesus, they had expected health to improve, bills to be paid, and doubts to disappear. Instead, life turned out to be painful, and sometimes God felt distant.

Such disillusionment may not compare to the shock felt by the disciples when Jesus died. Nevertheless, there is something of a dying experience in the lives of most Christians. Death and resurrection are lifelong themes of discipleship, not just aspects of the story of Jesus.

Between periods of dynamic spiritual growth, there may be times of drought. In some paradoxical way, desert experiences can prepare the way for spiritual growth. If distance runners never felt the pain of oxygen-starved muscles and the despair of poor performance, they would never grace the victory stand. If Christians never experience doubt, discouragement, and even anger at God, perhaps our faith has not yet met the test of real struggle with human limitations of acting and understanding.

Powerlessness and Anger

Ann told the story of her early experience as a Christian, when exuberant faith alternated with pain or anger. When she came to faith at the age of twenty-one, she was grappling with the racial and gender inequalities of South African society.

"One of my main preoccupations was my identity as a woman. Inequality was rife, and that didn't exclude the church. I had a deep sense of powerlessness and anger, even anger at God."

In her struggle, she sensed God asking her the very question he used when Job challenged God's goodness:

Where were you when I laid the foundation of the earth? Tell me,
if you have understanding. (Job 38:4)

Ann continued:

Although it's hard to explain concisely, there was a clear
moment when I was aware of my insignificance in the face
of God's grandeur, in the face of his power to create, in rela-
tion to time and space, and next to billions of other people
down through the centuries. Who was I?

Then I was overwhelmed by an incredible Presence. God
met me, and for two weeks I was on a strange high, as if
everything had a miraculous hue. A short while afterward,
when I was alone, I had a deep awareness of sin—a feeling of
the absence of God. This was a vital part of my understanding. It confirmed my need for God. I had always sought independence. At this point I was learning the act of surrender.

I gave over to God those things that I held onto tightly,
emotionally and intellectually, things that meant the most
to me. If God gave them back, I could accept them as a gift.
If not, they had loosened their grip on me and pushed me
forward in my learning.

One precious thing Ann said she gave up to God was grappling
for a place of significance *as a woman.* "I was keenly aware of all the
inequalities, imperfections, and misunderstandings around the
gender issue. But Christ had challenged his society's subordina-
tion of women," Ann said. "Jesus revolutionized the standing of
women, and each person was given their dignity and significance."

I observed a paradox in what Ann was saying: she gave up
fighting for her own rights as a woman in a patriarchal society,
and instead found identity and meaning in her relationship with
Christ. That spiritual grounding, in turn, gave her confidence

and freedom that enabled her to become a successful professional woman. Am I willing, I wondered, to give up the built-in advantages men often have in Western culture, and to base my identity wholly in a relationship with Christ?

Working in a risky situation raised another basic discipleship question for Ann: Was she willing to give even her life in order to work in the township set apart for blacks?

In the end, I decided I was willing, and then I was freed to work there. I was no longer bound by fear.

One week I was physically attacked twice. A man jumped into my car to steal my purse. Then a gang of four youth waited outside a school where I taught. As I drove by, they threw rocks and broke windows of my car. One boulder skimmed the back of my head. On both occasions, I learned later that a Christian friend had sensed that I was in danger, and was praying for me.

Ann reflected on the paradox of finding freedom in letting go of what seems most precious: "If you hold onto anything tightly—job, career, family, reputation—you are not really free for discipleship. It's in letting go of these, in giving them back to God, that God finally is able to use you."

By way of analogy, Ann remembered a difficult time before marriage when she and Nic were dating and their relationship had faltered.

We had moved apart. We had to give each other up and not cling tightly to the relationship. In the end, that experience of letting go prepared us for marriage. Periodically, I have to assess my relationships and my attitudes toward many areas of life, and once again give up everything to God.

Unless a grain of wheat falls into the earth and dies, it remains just a single grain; but if it dies, it bears much fruit. Those who love their life lose it. (John 12:24)

Prayer on Paper

Ever since his teen years, Nic has kept a journal—a discipline many people find helpful in their faith journey. "Journaling is therapy without a therapist; it is prayer on paper," he said.

Nic has covered a lot of terrain in his pilgrimage, from no explicit faith as a teenager, to fervent evangelical faith as a young adult, to a present period of reappraisal and questioning. Closely related to his faith story has been a lifelong, largely unrealized hope of making a living as a musician. Not long before we walked together, Nic read back through his journals and wrote summary observations about transition points in his life. He shared some of this written summary with me:

On the 10th January 1979, I was conscripted, by the scruff of my neck, into the South African Defense Force. Basic training was the worst time of my life, and meant that my privacy was assaulted like never before. This assault and battery was to "break open the alabaster jar" and cause me to take some real steps toward God and myself.

One of the most interesting things in retrospect was my keeping a little notebook with me at all times, into which I wrote wild and raw thoughts. It's as though my whole conversion process has been captured, as though I was a photojournalist at the scene of an historic occurrence. It was my first journaling, and it happened without any real knowledge of what that meant, no awareness of it as a discipline. . . .

Most of my recorded thoughts came out of the heat of the moment. With such bodily and mental constraints as the military enforces upon you, your spirit is squeezed and thoughts come squirting out.

Woven into the account of Nic's teenage and early adult years is a constant theme of passionate involvement in music. He learned to play several instruments, wrote many songs, and drew inspiration from various rock, jazz, and classical musicians. As an eighteen-year-old in the army, he also became a Christian:

Nic Paton reads from his journal.

I was standing guard for a four-hour Saturday afternoon shift, reading *Faith for Daily Living* magazine, and underlining the pertinent bits. I became aware of an imperative, . . . a voice calling without words, a question floating around me. I had the feeling that there was a line drawn in front of me which I was to cross, or a cliff or building's edge off of which I was to jump. . . . There was a subconscious argument going on inside of me. I said simply, "Okay, Lord, I'll go for it." That was it!

In a journal entry soon after his conversion, Nic wrote, "God, are you listening? I want to work out what I want to be, what I'm doing, what I must be, what I really am. What is a musician? I want to be one." That cry to God for identity became a focal point in his life, the center of much energy and pain in subsequent years.

"I was totally committed to music," Nic said as we crossed a meadow on the Pilgrims' Way. "For ten years I gave music to God in the church, often playing with a worship group that was not up to standards I wanted."

Poetry and Imagination

I recalled the first time I saw Nic. He was playing guitar and singing at an informal gathering of friends. Nic had command of the strings and sang with passion and skill. Later he loaned me recordings of music he had written and performed, songs full of poetry and imagination. He has a gift I can only dream of possessing, and he wanted to use that gift in service for God.

When Nic and Ann moved to London not long before Ellen and I met them, the plan was for Nic to make a living with his music. He gave guitar lessons and did some performing, but neither generated enough income to make the endeavor viable.

"For a long time," he said, "creativity was the measure of my faith. Now I can't escape the idea that I'm a failed artist. I'm not looking to be well-known; I just want to make a contribution and use my abilities."

There was no bitterness in Nic's voice, just the pain of someone who sought to use his artistic abilities for God and ended up feeling spent and unfulfilled. "When I became a Christian as a young adult, I went to church happily for several years. Today I have only marginal involvement in the church. I'm no longer interested in labels or confessions."

I asked Nic if, reflecting on his own faith pilgrimage, he would offer any counsel to new believers. He replied:

> In the stage of early belief, new Christians should be made aware that it won't always be that simple. Early on as a Christian, I became convinced that there is a place in faith for the arts. For years I tried to live that out. I believe that conviction was God-given, but it brought me a lot of pain. Too often Christians idealize simple faith—and then meet complex situations where a "simple faith" isn't adequate.

Wrestling with Angels

I had a sense of walking on holy ground as Nic said these painful things. He is past playing games with God, unwilling or unable to pretend his faith burns brightly. I thought of other God-seekers who have had long stretches in the desert.

Moses was in the wilderness, far from his spiritual roots and his family in Egypt, until God spoke to him in a burning bush (Exodus 3). Elijah was fleeing exhausted and disillusioned to Mount Horeb, where God was not in the fire or the wind but finally spoke after Elijah waited for the "sound of sheer silence" (1 Kings 19:12). Jesus was tempted and tormented alone in the desert, until "angels came and attended to his needs" (Matthew 4:11, REB).

All three faced into the unknown of the wilderness, wrestled with their doubts and fears and pain. All three emerged stronger for the tasks ahead.

One of my favorite Bible stories is the account of Jacob wrestling with a spiritual being on the night before he met his long-estranged twin brother Esau. Jacob had wronged Esau and had spent many years in a foreign country because of that. Now it was the night before he planned to meet Esau again:

> *Jacob was left alone; and a man wrestled with him until daybreak. When the man saw that he did not prevail against Jacob,*

he struck him on the hip socket; and Jacob's hip was put out of joint as he wrestled with him. Then he said, "Let me go, for the day is breaking." But Jacob said, "I will not let you go, unless you bless me." So he said to him, "What is your name?" And he said, "Jacob." Then the man said, "You shall no longer be called Jacob, but Israel, for you have striven with God and with humans, and have prevailed." Then Jacob asked him, "Please tell me your name." But he said, "Why is it that you ask my name?" And there he blessed him. So Jacob called the place Peniel ["The face of God"], saying, "For I have seen God face to face, and yet my life is preserved." The sun rose upon him as he passed Penuel, limping because of his hip. (Genesis 32:24-31)

I believe on that mysterious night of the soul, Jacob wrestled with doubt, fear, guilt, and basic questions about his identity. This struggle came many years after he put his trust in God. It was not the immature thrashings of a babe in faith. What Jacob needed was a blessing from God, an unmistakable signal that God cared about him and would give him a meaningful identity.

Out of that ferocious struggle, Jacob finally received a blessing. He also received a new identity in the name *Israel,* meaning "He strives with God," and a wounded hip that probably gave him a limp for the rest of his life.

Waymarks of a Spiritual Direction

In the years leading up to our time on the Pilgrims' Way, Nic wrestled in the wilderness, feeling the earth move under his faith footing. But within his own journal entries are waymarks of a spiritual direction that will guide Nic as he moves forward. He has an instinctive distrust of dogma, a desire to "see the face of God" without the trappings of religious systems and institutions:

Life is a dynamic process. So to make it into a philosophy or theology . . . is to go against its intrinsic nature, and it dies.

Maybe this is what kids know. . . . Little children are chaotic beings, raw and unsophisticated. The Spirit of God, I believe, makes us into disciplined and mature beings, but wants us to enjoy, experience, and communicate the rawness of energy which has not been ossified into a system.

Herein lies great freedom. It is indeed impossible to crawl back into your mother's womb and become an actual child—although you would think some people thought so in their misguided admonishments to blind, childish "faith." And yet faith can only take place when one relocates away from the safe center of being to its edges, where one allows the world out there to encounter us and create new experiences. . . .

[The rock musician] Sting talked about how at the outset, young musicians who are generally poor and struggling are concerned about survival, the things of the street. They talk in very raw and direct terms. As they gain success, they begin to lead a comfortable and sheltered life, and their writing gets more abstract. It may lose the edge, and in the end they have nothing to say at all.

Referring to hazards encountered by young believers, Nic reflected on his ultimately unsatisfying years of participation in a congregation and Bible college where answers were provided and questions were discouraged.

"The problem lay not so much in what was taught at face value, but in the underlying, *unanalyzed* philosophy and assumed value system" of people in that community. Nic was in a fellowship that did not encourage him to think and probe. Eventually he threw off the constraints of that community, and with it much of their belief system. He still is struggling to reestablish a life-giving way of relating to God.

Brilliant Light and Deep Shadow

I have come to see doubt as the necessary shadow side of faith. A good photograph or painting often has areas of both brilliant light and deep shadow. Take away shadows, and the picture disappears. The same is true for Christian faith and discipleship. There's no need to try to generate doubts or painful questions. These will emerge in the ordinary life of any thinking person.

Some individuals or churches try to avoid the awkwardness of doubt by setting a rigid standard of what must be done or believed. I am all for individuals and churches defining a clear confession of faith or naming specific patterns of discipleship that will guide daily life. But that can only be life-giving if there also is an environment in which it is acceptable to test, question, and evaluate.

There are moments when I ask foundational questions about my faith: How do I know that Jesus is the Son of God? How could I prove to myself and others that God even exists? How do I know the resurrection happened? To ignore such questions is to have faith gradually drift away from intellectual moorings. To articulate such questions, and talk them over with other believers, is to use God-given mental faculties to build a stronger base of understanding.

I need a community and I need Christian friends who are not unsettled by critical reflection on what Christians often take for granted. When my faith is strong and I have unbounded conviction of God's reality and love, then I can be a source of strength to others. When doubt shakes my foundations, others can provide a refuge of acceptance and hope that restores my confidence.

My awareness of God varies from day to day. Here and there throughout my life, though, there have been times when I have known God's presence in unmistakable ways:

• At a time of prayer on the night before our wedding.

• At the birth of our second daughter, after half a year of threatened miscarriage.

• In the struggle to find direction at career crossroads.

• In the sustaining power of God's love when I was physically or emotionally exhausted and had important tasks to finish.

Such experiences give me a memory of God's faithfulness to draw upon in times of doubt or discouragement.

Stages of Faith Development

Ann began to reflect on her reading of a book called *God of Surprises,* in which author Gerard Hughes describes three common stages of faith development:

1. Many Christians begin at an *institutional* stage of faith, in which like infants we are dependent upon structures provided by others for our very survival. Whether we actually are children learning the Bible at Sunday school, or adult new believers learning the basics of Christian faith, we accept what trustworthy mentors provide for us.

2. We move on to a *critical* stage, in which like adolescents we challenge, probe, and even reject. We question and doubt, sort out what holds true to our own experience, and become aware of the limits of certainty in matters of faith.

3. Eventually we come to a *mystical* stage, when we become deeply aware of the mystery of God's presence within us. Prayer includes silence and fellowship with God rather than simply our words, and we become conscious of our deepest fears, hopes, and needs.

All three of the above stages are necessary for Christian growth. All three must function side-by-side in the mature believer. We need the structure and accountability of a faith community (the institutional aspect). We must continue to apply the best resources of intellect and reason to what we believe (the critical aspect). We also need the energy and awe that come from awareness of God's presence (the mystical aspect).

In some sense we move through these stages of faith development just as our physical bodies move from infancy, through adolescence, to adulthood. But discipleship is most life-giving when it eventually includes a childlike reliance on the faith community, a keen intellect to ask questions, and a heart warmed by divine companionship.

Prayer Partners

For two years Ellen and Ann had met weekly to compare notes on their spiritual life and pray together. "This has been life-giving for me," Ellen offered. "I find I can carry joys and concerns better during the week if I know I can bring them to our time of prayer. We laugh and cry together. Our exchange is confidential and often very personal."

Over coffee the two women talked about what was happening in their lives, articulated worries or hopes, and prayed. Ann laughed as she shared:

It is more than just cappuccino! We pray about work, about current events, about people we love. We don't try to be pious with each other or with God. We can be earthy, intellectual, playful, or angry. We are honest with each other and bring that honesty to God.

We keep a notebook and write down what we have prayed about. A week later we come back and report what God has done, and give thanks.

Ellen and Ann explained that their prayer is a simple matter of "lifting concerns to God." They recommend books to each other, talk about dreams, and give one another a place for con-

Ellen with her prayer partner, Ann Paton

fession. "When I go through a bad experience," Ann acknowledged, "our prayer time is a lifeline."

Ellen and Ann got started meeting at a time when Ann was
seeking a prayer partner. "A mutual friend recommended Ellen
to me," she said. There was something of a divine appointment
in that new friendship. "The right person must be God-given,"
Ann commented thoughtfully. "Then you must walk alongside
that individual. Often that's the only thing you can do for a
prayer partner: walk with them as a sign of God's faithfulness."

New Life from a Dead Tree

In late afternoon our dirt path through the birches and pas-
tures came to an end. We walked down a mile of blacktopped
road into the picturesque village of Chilham. As we approached
the hamlet, two swans swooped low overhead, gaining altitude

after takeoff from the grounds of Chilham Castle. Their long necks and huge wingspan made an impressive sight.

Only a few hundred people live in the cluster of crooked old houses in the village, around a wide open square. We passed the fifteenth-century White Horse Pub and followed the Pilgrims' Way down a side street to St. Mary's Church. Like many churches in southeastern England, this one is built of flint stone, "hard as the devil's toenail," in the local lore.

I had read about a *seventh-century* yew tree beside St. Mary's Church at Chilham, and in the fading light we sought it out. To my disappointment, we found nothing but an eight-foot-wide stump of ragged and gnarled dead wood, jutting ten or twelve feet toward the sky, surrounded by a metal fence. Town residents informed us that the precious tree had survived thirteen centuries, only to be blown down in the great windstorm of 1987. A tree surgeon had raised hopes that new life would sprout from the tangle of broken timber. But almost a decade later, there is no sign of renewal.

I asked if anyone had thought to preserve a seedling, and was told that none survived. It is virtually certain, however, that birds and wind had dispersed seeds far and wide for many centuries. There may be hundreds of yews descended from that one dead tree, even if the lineage is not recognized or celebrated.

Mature discipleship is like a great yew tree—harboring life, reaching toward heaven in praise of the Creator, providing shade to weary travelers, and offering a refuge for children's play. Storms can destroy a great tree, but out of the dying branches and scattered debris, God will raise up new seedlings of joy, love, and hope.

Prayer

Out of the depths I cry to you, O Lord.
   Lord, hear my voice!
Let your ears be attentive
   to the voice of my supplications!
If you, O Lord, should mark iniquities,
   Lord, who could stand?
But there is forgiveness with you,
   so that you may be revered.
I wait for [you], my soul waits,
   and in [your] word I hope;
my soul waits for [you]
   more than those who watch for the morning,
   more than those who watch for the morning.

(from Psalm 130)

For Reflection

1. What questions or life experiences have most tested your faith in God or your commitment to follow Jesus? Where did you find help or encouragement to carry on?

2. What part do periods of doubt or spiritual drought play in your walk with God? Is there any pattern to when they come? After a time of growth or ecstatic experience? After an experience of loss or shame?

3. Can you name personal goals or ambitions that you have needed to abandon? What emotions or feelings accompanied the process of letting go? Did your relationship with God play a part in how or why you let go? Did you wrestle with God as Jacob did?

4. Do the three stages of faith development, as described by Gerard Hughes, make sense to you? Can you identify examples of all three in your own life (past or present)? Do you wish to have one or two of the stages more evident in your present

faith journey?

5. Have you ever prayed regularly with a partner? In what ways do you think such a commitment would be helpful or unhelpful?

10

Rely on the Holy Spirit

Pentecost Sunday morning, May 26
Chilham to Canterbury (6 miles)
Fellow pilgrims: Brother Damon Kelly, Ellen Kraybill

Following Jesus may mean giving up wealth and status •
The gospel is foolishness in the eyes of those who don't
know Jesus • Prayer books and other worship aids may be useful
in a regular prayer life • The Holy Spirit enables us to remember
and live out the example and teachings of Jesus • The Spirit
gives diverse gifts, which do not reflect spiritual status •
Love is the greatest spiritual gift • Following Jesus
may require us to resist pressure from government
or society to conform.

Six Miles from Canterbury

The smell of freshly brewed coffee wafted up from the kitchen
when Ellen and I awoke in Chilham on Sunday morning. We
were in the sixteenth-century ivy-covered Bagham Farm House,
with its six lofty chimney pots and steep red tile roof. Floors
around us had a gentle tilt, and windows with a dozen diamond-
shaped leaded panes let in the dawn light.

This was Pentecost Sunday, when Christians celebrate the
first great outpouring of the Holy Spirit on believers at Jerusalem
(Acts 2). By any conventional practice of pilgrimage, this Sunday

should have been the last day of my journey: Canterbury was a mere six miles away. I intended to walk one day further to the Bruderhof community at Nonington. But for the moment I was eager to get to the walled city that attracts Christians from around the world.

Our hosts at the farmhouse gave us an early breakfast, since we planned to leave in time to reach Canterbury for an 11:00 a.m. service. We ate a sumptuous hot meal on sturdy wooden tables next to a walk-in sized fireplace. Oak beams sagged so low above us I could not stand up fully at one end of the room.

A Franciscan Brother at the Door

Just before 8:00 a.m., there was a knock on the door. In stepped Brother Damon, a Franciscan friar in his midthirties who would join Ellen and me for our walk into Canterbury. In his long chocolate-brown habit, with a white rope belt and sandals, Brother Damon made an imposing figure.

He and I had corresponded about his interest in Mennonites, but this was the first time we had met. A small modern rucksack looked incongruous against his medieval attire. With laughing eyes, Damon apologized for not being barefoot.

There was no time to waste. The three of us set out for Canterbury at a brisk pace. Beyond the little village of Old Wives Lees, we passed fields with hundreds of tall poles and a maze of wires used to support vines of the climbing hop plant. The hop flower gives a much-desired bitter flavor to the lagers, stouts, and other beverages for which southeast England is famous. Long lines of tall poplar trees line the edges of the hop fields, protecting the delicate flowers from strong winds.

Farms and villages mostly were still asleep on Sunday morning, but the sight of a robed friar turned a few heads as we made our way to Canterbury. Early in the thirteenth century, Francis of Assisi wore the sackcloth habit as a sign of repentance and humility after his conversion to radical Christianity.

He was the son of a wealthy cloth merchant in the Italian city of Assisi. Francis had every possible advantage to make his life comfortable. But on a pilgrimage to Rome, he was moved to compassion by the suffering of beggars. He exchanged his fine clothes for the rags of a penniless man and spent a day begging.

Francis was transformed by this experience of poverty and powerlessness. He resolved to abandon his wealth and serve the poor. Disowned by his parents, Francis devoted himself to helping lepers. He worshiped at a small church near Assisi, and heard the Gospel text read in which Jesus says:

> *As you go, proclaim the good news, "The kingdom of heaven has come near." Cure the sick, raise the dead, cleanse the lepers, cast out demons. You received without payment; give without payment. Take no gold, or silver, or copper in your belts, no bag for your journey, or two tunics, or sandals, or a staff. . . .*
> (Matthew 10:7-10)

Taking this as a personal call, Francis put on a long dark robe and discarded even his staff and shoes. Soon a small band of fellow pilgrims joined his radical quest to follow Jesus, and the Franciscan Order was born. Rules for the order (the *Regula Primitiva*) were based on simple teachings of the Gospels. With his love for people and nature, Francis inspired a missionary movement that soon spread across Europe.

Brother Damon explained,

Lepers in Francis' day were outcasts and had to wear special clothes. Francis had a great fear of lepers before his conversion. They represented sickness, death, and abandonment by God. Then the Lord told Francis to embrace a leper. He got off his horse, ran, and kissed a leper. This was the big

Brother Damon, wearing the traditional habit of a Franciscan brother

breakthrough to his conversion. This was acting like Jesus, who emptied himself and took on the whole of human suffering and sin.

Pointing to his own robe, Damon said, "Francis designed this habit to look like what the lepers wore." Damon was quick to add that putting on a robe was the easiest part of his own experience in discipleship. "What you wear is only the beginning; obedience to Christ must be your whole life."

Work with the Homeless

Working with the homeless in Canterbury and London has been brother Damon's calling in recent years. "Often the homeless are people who have not known love, either as children or as adults," he observed. "They sometimes are angry and don't understand love. Like Jesus on the cross, they cry out to God, 'Why have you forsaken me?' [Mark 15:34].

"Homeless people sometimes see me on the street in my habit and call out abuse, showing their hurt and confusion."

Damon quoted an ancient hymn about Jesus:

> *Let the same mind be in you that was in Christ Jesus,*
> *   who, though he was in the form of God,*
> *   did not regard equality with God*
> *   as something to be exploited,*
> *   but emptied himself,*
> *   taking the form of a slave,*
> *   being born in human likeness.*
> *And being found in human form,*
> *   he humbled himself*
> *   and became obedient to the point of death—*
> *   even death on a cross. (Philippians 2:5-8)*

Damon expounded the text:

> Jesus emptied himself and became one with suffering humanity. God became a victim of his own love. In Jesus, God was reaching out to a broken world. The church is made up of broken people; we are all disjointed, and we all need love. The apostle Paul said, "The whole creation has been groaning in labor pains" [Romans 8:22]. Most of the homeless people I work with have had something go wrong with their family: parents alienated from each other, abortion, broken relationships, destruction of life in one way or another.

Ever quick to laugh at himself, Damon described what it's like to wear a friar's habit in the streets of Britain. "Schoolchildren—or even groups of workmen—sometimes laugh at us. We set ourselves up for it! If I were a schoolboy and saw a man in a brown dress . . ." Here Damon doubled over with merriment and observed:

> The hood and the habit look silly. We are foolish in the eyes
> of the world. The gospel is foolishness in the world's eyes—
> but it is the wisdom of God. The apostle Paul said, "We have
> become a spectacle to the world, to angels and to mortals"
> [1 Corinthians 4:9]. But there is great joy in the gospel, in
> being one with the Lord even in his sufferings.

A Memory Device for Use in Prayer

Suspended from brother Damon's belt was a large string of rosary beads, something that my own Anabaptist tradition usually has treated as foolishness. Two years earlier, an elderly Catholic sister in Dublin had explained to me that the rosary consists of fifty beads divided into five "decades" of ten each. The sister used the rosary in prayer and meditation, with each bead reminding her of one aspect of the story of Jesus.

First come the "joyful mysteries," fifty verses or incidents from the story of Jesus' birth. These are followed by the "sorrowful mysteries," fifty aspects of Jesus' suffering and death. Finally come the fifty "glorious mysteries" of events related to the resurrection of Jesus and the role of Mary.

Catholics pray to Mary (and to other saints); most Protestants do not. This has been a long-standing source of debate between Christians. The rosary beads in particular have been associated with prayers to Mary, since the Catholic convention is to insert a forty-two word "Hail Mary" prayer between every one of the fifty beads.

My understanding of Scripture and my experience of Jesus do not lead me to pray to Mary. It's unlikely that traditional use of rosary beads could become part of my own prayer life. What fascinates me about the rosary, though, is that it serves as a memory device to reflect on the birth, death, and resurrection of Jesus. Someone who really knows the rosary "mysteries" can retell and meditate upon 150 aspects of the Jesus story.

Not all Christians warm to the idea of praying with a string of beads, but some memory device may be helpful to plant biblical stories in the mind. My family and I once learned the Beatitudes (Matthew 5:1-12) by inventing gestures to accompany each verse. Learning Scripture became a playful exercise, and physical motion seemed to reinforce memory.

Brother Damon mentioned that Franciscans routinely meditate on Gospel passages, visualizing the stories of Jesus as if they themselves were there. "I try to imagine, for example, what it would have been like to be a brother of Jesus," Damon said.

I mentioned that I have been nurtured by biblical storytelling—learning Bible stories just as they are written, interpreting them with good expression and a few gestures. Whatever the method, it is life-transforming to be immersed both in Bible stories and other narratives of God's faithfulness.

Part of Brother Damon's discipline is to pause five times each day for "offices" of prayer and Bible reading. As we walked, he pulled from his rucksack a breviary (prayer book) that has daily assigned readings and prayers—including psalms for each of the five offices. The breviary gets Damon through the Psalms once a month, and through much of the Bible once a year.

In my own experience I've found it helpful to use a "one-year Bible" plan. It structures my daily worship so that I always have one reading each from the Old Testament, the Gospels, the New Testament letters, and the Psalms. The plan I use has one set of readings for every day of the year, so I always know what to read. If I fall behind in the plan, I allow myself to skip a few chapters and then read what is assigned for a given calendar day.

Without a reading plan, I discovered, I was likely to become discouraged and hesitate to recover the pattern of daily reading.

That might not be good enough for me to be a friar, but it's kept me at regular Bible reading!

A Merry Entry into Canterbury

Suddenly we realized that conversation was slowing down our walking. We began to worry that we would not arrive at Canterbury in time for Ellen and me to attend the eleven o'clock cathedral service. We picked up our pace and began joking about someday just barely making it into heaven on time.

In heaven, we decided, we'll run into sinners like ourselves who are chuckling and saying, "You know, I'm not really supposed to be here!"

A significant part of the medieval city wall still surrounds Canterbury, encircling the magnificent cathedral and a labyrinth of narrow streets. At a brisk walk we entered by the arched West Gate and made our way up a long pedestrian street of shops and restaurants. We hurried past the venerable Eastbridge Hospital (hospice), where pilgrims to Canterbury have found food and lodging since the year 1190.

Ellen and I were headed for an Anglican worship service, so Brother Damon peeled off down a side street to Catholic mass at the Franciscan House. Ellen and I entered the cathedral grounds through the medieval Christ Church Gate, which is squeezed into a crowded row of shops and houses.

Because I had corresponded with them about my walking project, cathedral staff members knew we were coming and ushered us into the long, majestic building. Organ notes cascaded through the ancient arches as the head steward took us to seats of honor at the front of twelve hundred Pentecost worshipers. We sat with thirty other dignitaries and guests just below and to the side of the high altar, feeling a bit self-conscious with our walking clothes, muddy shoes, and rucksacks.

The wife of the cathedral canon (a clergyman with adminis-

The final approach to Canterbury Cathedral is through narrow, ancient streets.

trative duties) sat nearby. She was dressed in elegant red, the liturgical color for Pentecost, and reached over to give us a warm handshake. We were facing across the nave, and on the opposite side sat an international group of Anglican, Catholic, and Orthodox church leaders.

The front two or three rows of the main seating area were filled with physically or mentally handicapped people from the L'Arche Community. On one side of the front row, in festive ceremonial attire, sat the lord mayor of Canterbury, with his mace perched before him on a special holder.

With the organ playing at full volume, a choir of twelve men and eighteen boys—all in white and violet robes—processed down the center aisle. At the head of the train, a woman in red and yellow carried a silver cross, followed by two people bearing candles. This being Pentecost, the vast congregation stood and sang,

> *Come down, O love divine, seek thou this soul of mine,*
> *and visit it with thine own ardor glowing;*
> *O Comforter, draw near, within my heart appear,*
> *and kindle it, thy holy flame bestowing.*

We knelt for confession of sin, heard the choir several times, and had a moment of silence. Then we listened to the words of Jesus, spoken the night before his crucifixion, when he described the role the Holy Spirit would have after Jesus was gone:

> *If you love me, you will keep my commandments. And I will ask the Father, and he will give you another Advocate, to be with you forever. This is the Spirit of truth. . . .*
> *I will not leave you orphaned; I am coming to you. In a little while the world will no longer see me, but you will see me; because I live, you also will live. . . .*
> *But the Advocate, the Holy Spirit, whom the Father will send*

in my name, will teach you everything, and remind you of all that I have said to you. (John 14:15-26)

The dean of the Cathedral, the senior residential minister responsible for worship and program, ascended to a lofty pulpit and preached in measured tones. For us, he said, the Holy Spirit is the key person of the Trinity. The Spirit is God active in the world today, "the originator of everything that has the gleam of truth." The Spirit will bring a sensitivity to people and their needs. The Spirit is not just confined to Christians, and does not compel us to act in a predetermined way.

Power to Live Like Jesus

The high-octane part of the sermon lay in a few brief comments about the Spirit transforming us into the likeness of Christ. The preacher didn't highlight this point, but I could not help but notice that Jesus speaks of the Holy Spirit in the context of obedience: "You will keep my commandments, and the Father will send an Advocate who will teach you everything and remind you of all that I have said to you" (my paraphrase).

The Spirit gives us power to live like Christ and points us back to the example and teaching of Jesus! The Spirit is no taskmaster, loading us with guilt for our inability to measure up: the word translated "Advocate" also means Comforter, Helper, Encourager, and Mediator.

In this empowering and supporting role, the Spirit enables us to live out the surprising and unsettling teachings of Jesus. With the divine Encourager, we are able to love our enemies, speak the truth, worry less about material security, keep our lives free from dishonorable relationships, and otherwise follow the example of Jesus.

At Pentecost, the first Christian community at Jerusalem had spectacular signs of the Holy Spirit's presence:

*And suddenly from heaven there came a sound like the rush of a
violent wind, and it filled the entire house where they were sitting. Divided tongues, as of fire, appeared among them, and a
tongue rested on each of them. All of them were filled with the
Holy Spirit and began to speak in other languages, as the Spirit
gave them ability.* (Acts 2:2-4)

In every generation since that day, some Christians have experienced unusual happenings attributed to the Holy Spirit. These
include speaking in tongues, interpreting the meaning of tongues,
offering words of spiritual insight, healing, and prophesying.

In addition to such startling gifts of the Spirit, there are seemingly ordinary gifts such as teaching, preaching, administration,
and hospitality. At the early church in the Greek city of Corinth,
the mix of activities and gifts being used became chaotic and
even divisive. In 1 Corinthians 12–14, the apostle Paul gives the
Corinthian Christians some needed counsel:

1. The Spirit gives a variety of gifts, and they should be
used for the *common good* of the church (12:4-11).

2. Believers should not feel superior or inferior because of
the particular gifts and abilities the Spirit has given them
(12:12-31).

3. Love for others is the greatest fruit of the Spirit, the required ingredient for expressing any gift (13:1-13; Galatians
5:22-23).

4. Speaking in tongues (which had become divisive at
Corinth) should happen in the gathered church only when
there is a meaningful interpretation of what is being said
(14:1-25). The tongues to which Paul refers may have been
random syllables also common in charismatic churches
today, not actual identifiable languages as described by Acts
2 for the first Pentecost Sunday.

5. Prophecy (speaking a message inspired by God to the congregation) is a gift that many Christians possess (14:26-39). Paul (or his readers?) apparently did not expect that women would immediately speak out in church, perhaps because women who previously attended Jewish synagogues would not have had biblical and theological training typical for men (14:34-36). Paul assumes, however, that both men and women will exercise leadership (11:4; Romans 16:1), fulfilling the ancient prophecy of Joel (Joel 2:28-29; Acts 2:17-18).

6. Worship should happen "decently and in order" (1 Corinthians 14:40).

Christians sometimes become divided over use and expression of Holy Spirit gifts, perhaps a sign that they are missing the most important gift or fruit of all—love. I have learned over the years to relax and enjoy the variety of ways people experience God. As a young man, I began to speak in tongues in private prayer before I ever heard anyone else use that gift. That has not made my experience of God superior to that of anyone else, only different.

Since then, I have learned that linguists can replicate the sounds and rhythms of the typical tongues speaker. I believe speaking in tongues is a natural human ability that God sometimes activates during times of worship.

I have deeply felt the presence of God in churches where there was well-planned liturgy, silence, carefully crafted sermons—and no tongues or any spectacular manifestations of the Spirit. I also have been very aware of God in churches where people spoke in tongues, laid hands on each other for healing, and spoke spontaneously.

Hence, I am slow to judge or condemn the spiritual gifts of others. I refuse to feel guilty because I don't have certain gifts. God delights in diversity, as long as worship is honorable and life-giving. In the end, what really matters is changed lives. We ask whether any particular spiritual gift or mode of worship enables participants to become more like Jesus in their day-to-day lives.

Vulnerable People at the Communion Table

Members of the L'Arche community, seated at the front of Canterbury Cathedral, were the first to take communion on Pentecost Sunday. I watched the faces of those vulnerable people, some of whom had severe mental and physical handicaps. They were eager and expectant. A few called out with joyful sounds as they grasped the cup. People whom society often pushes to the margins found delight in taking part in this remembrance of Christ's broken body.

Canon Peter Brett, a senior minister who helps direct the cathedral's life and witness, gave us a gracious greeting after the service. He stood in the cathedral transept, where the two naves of the massive building intersect, and talked with us warmly for fifteen minutes.

Now that worshipers had left, crowds of tourists brushed by us to see the building. Canon Brett kept a keen eye open for caps on the heads of men, and politely signaled for any such to be removed.

We moved to the exact spot in the north transept of the cathedral where Archbishop Thomas Becket was murdered in 1170. That is the event that soon brought thousands of pilgrims streaming to Canterbury from across Europe. "Thomas was tweaking the nose of the king," Canon Brett noted. "He was almost seeking martyrdom—the sacrifice of the individual for his conviction."

Armed men loyal to the king pursued Thomas into the cathedral, where a knight named Richard the Brett swung a sword that shattered the archbishop's skull. "The knight had my own surname, I'm afraid," Canon Brett said with a wry smile.

I asked Canon Brett if he thought there are times today when

Canturbury Cathedral as seen from Christ Church Gate

church leaders should stand up to political rulers. He thought a moment, then said, "Perhaps the Falklands War was a time when the church needed to speak." He was recalling the time a decade earlier when Argentina seized South Atlantic islands long claimed by Britain. The two nations fought a short but bloody war.

At that time, the Archbishop of Canterbury said the British needed forgiveness as much as the Argentinians—and Prime Minister Thatcher didn't like that. In relations between church and state, we need the courage of our convictions. There are other issues to which the church must speak: genetic engineering, unemployed young people on the streets, inadequate housing in the inner cities, political prisoners around the world.

With that, Canon Brett left us, wishing me well on the rest of my walk. Ellen and I had lunch together, then walked to Canterbury station, where she took a train back to London. In my mind was the prospect of meeting more Franciscans and joining a Pentecost feast. I made my way across town to the friary to which Brother Damon had directed me.

Prayer

I am amazed, O God, that your Son Jesus emptied himself of status and became like the lowliest servant among ordinary men and women. I struggle with even small steps toward vulnerability and service. Let your Holy Spirit flood my life like a mighty river, washing away pride and nurturing deep roots of love for you and compassion for others. Let me open my life to worship that will help me grow in you. Show me how your Spirit can use gifts I have for the work of your kingdom. Amen.

For Reflection

1. Why do you think God called Francis of Assisi to give up his wealth and work among the poor? What is it about the poor (us?) that makes them responsive to God? What is it about wealth that could make it hard for the rich (us?) to be aware of God?

2. Have you found ways to incorporate poetry, music, art, or drama into worship? What might be the advantages and disadvantages of using prayer books and other worship aids?

3. What gifts of the Holy Spirit do you most yearn to express in your own life? What gifts have you seen among other Christians? Do these gifts seem to make people live more like Jesus?

4. What political or social issues today do you think might require followers of Jesus to resist pressure from government or society? What matters of obedience to God would be worth dying for?

Value One Another

Pentecost Sunday p.m., May 26: Canterbury
Hosts: Capuchin friars of the Franciscan order

Each individual has worth in the eyes of God • It is liberating to share possessions • Sexual status is not the deepest defining identity for Christians • All members of a Christian community give and receive counsel from each other • The Holy Spirit enables people of many different backgrounds to live and work together • Jesus gives practical steps for how to deal with conflict • The Spirit of Jesus is uniquely present when we work at conflict issues • Prayer is the process of bringing all aspects of ourselves and the world to God • The Psalms model complete candor in prayer.

At Home with the Friars

I rang the doorbell at a large house near Canterbury Cathedral where a small sign read "The Capuchins." This name is derived from the Italian word for the hood worn by Franciscan friars. In 1525 the Anabaptist renewal movement to which I belong started in Switzerland. In that same year, the Capuchin renewal movement began in Italy within the well-established Franciscan Order of the Roman Catholic Church.

Today some twelve thousand Capuchin friars (brothers) in seventy-six countries have taken vows of poverty, chastity, and obedience to Christ. Brother Damon, who walked with Ellen and

Capuchin House of the Franciscan order, near Canterbury Cathedral

me into Canterbury, is a member of the Capuchin branch of the Franciscan Order.

Brother Damon opened the door and showed me to a small, sparsely furnished room where I would spend the night. Then he introduced me to several other friars and invited me to join them for conversation in the front room.

According to local lore, the brothers said, their sixteenth-century house in Canterbury was variously a tavern, a brothel, a prison, and a private dwelling before becoming a friary in 1980. Presently eight friars are in residence, mostly engaged in practical ministry and in training at the nearby Franciscan Study Centre. Individually, they work in a prison, at a hospice for the dying, at a hospital, in a primary school, at the L'Arche Community, at a day center for the poor, and at a soup kitchen for the homeless.

God Treasures Each Individual

Brother Peter served me tea. He is a burly middle-aged man who made me think of the outspoken fisherman who followed Jesus. We fell into conversation, and I learned that he was trained as a nurse. As a young man, he had joined the navy and worked on a nuclear submarine that cruised off the coast of Russia.

At that time Peter was seeking to know God and to do something that would value human life. He became part of a justice and peace group at his home church in England during leave from submarine duty. Eventually he also worked with a victim support project, standing with people who were the targets of crime.

These experiences awakened Peter to the need for the gospel both in the world and in his own life. He said,

> Our Western society has lost the sense that each individual has worth and that creation is something to be valued and protected. We have a society based on death. We bump off the elderly, bump off the unwanted child, bump off our political enemies.

A deepening relationship with God transformed Peter.

> When you realize that God values you, then you value yourself—and that gets reflected in how you value others. You can't throw nuclear bombs or have an abortion when you see how much God treasures each individual.

Peter described how a local schizophrenic man regularly comes to the door of the friary at Canterbury and says, "I have something very important to tell you." The brothers invite him in, and he repeats a familiar pattern of scattered conversation.

"We simply treat him with dignity, and show him the love of

Christ," Peter explained. He lamented the fact that our society often measures individual worth in terms of salary or material possessions:

> You *are* somebody if you have wealth. In America, the rich drive around in limousines half a mile long, for the whole world to see! Jesus says that every person has worth. That's what I try to communicate now in my work with prisoners. My main task in life is to make others realize their value.

The Discipline of Commitment

I asked the brothers what was most difficult about their vows of poverty, celibacy, and obedience. Poverty was not the biggest challenge, they said—at least not after they had made the initial commitment to live with virtually no personal possessions.

Brother Andrew, speaking with a melodious Scottish accent, gave a simple illustration of how the Franciscan community handles property: "If you buy a book for personal study, you put it into the house library when you are finished."

Peter said he bought a Walkman so he could play language tapes to learn German, but other friars borrow it to listen to music tapes. "Such possessions aren't *mine*," he declared. "They are *ours*."

Andrew added that he has a set of watercolors which give him an artistic outlet. "Especially in celibate life, you need a creative outlet."

Mention of celibacy brought up the aspect of a friar's life that most often raises questions in modern society. The brothers were quick to emphasize that celibacy is not a universal ideal for all Christians. But it is a discipline and way of life to which they have been called. One of their brochures gave this summary of the logic of celibacy:

Married love has for its purpose the forming of an exclusive human relationship. When a person chooses to be celibate, he decides to give up that kind of relationship. He chooses another kind of relationship, one which directs itself to God in such a way that it can be given deeply and caringly, though not exclusively, to all men and women.

I admired the conviction and fortitude of these men. They have voluntarily relinquished a kind of intimacy that our society has virtually made a requirement for personal fulfillment. Prevailing values would have us believe that genital activity is a fundamental right of existence, that we must allow free expression of almost any sexual inclination.

Jesus rejected such a drives-based approach to sexuality, calling his followers to self-discipline even with the imagination (Matthew 5:27-30). Early Christians understood sexual intercourse, in a covenant relationship between husband and wife, to be so good a thing that they compared the intimacy of marriage to the relationship between Christ and the church (2 Corinthians 11:2; Ephesians 5:25-33; Revelation 19:7).

Yet the apostle Paul knew that the expectations of a spouse and family would not give some followers of Jesus the freedom to live out their calling (1 Corinthians 7:32-35). Whether married or celibate, I am convinced, Christians must never allow sexual status to become our deepest defining identity. Nor can we allow sexual desires to become a preoccupation that governs our lives.

The most difficult aspect of a friar's life is neither poverty nor celibacy, the brothers said, but obedience. Day after day in service to God, they voluntarily give their time, talents, and energy to the mission of the community. They are like musicians in an orchestra, who realize that the skill of each musician reaches full potential in finding harmony with other performers under the direction of an able conductor. In a world that idealizes individualism, such a commitment to group accountability is a rare thing.

The apostle Paul counseled Christians to be "subject to one another out of reverence for Christ" (Ephesians 5:21). Paul described a reciprocal relationship in which all members of a faith community are able to give and receive counsel and guidance. Such accountability applies to all believers, whether we live in the same household or simply gather each week for worship and fellowship. We need the wisdom and spiritual discernment of other Christians in large and small matters of our daily lives.

Shared Solitude with God

At 6:00 p.m. conversations ceased. All brothers in the household climbed creaking stairs to a chapel in the attic for ninety minutes of evening prayer. In a semicircle we sat with unstructured silence in the simple loft, under aged roof rafters. On a table before us, two candles burned.

Half an hour into prayer time, the mighty bells of Canterbury Cathedral began to peel just a few hundred feet away—close enough that we could hear noises of pulleys and ropes animating the chimes. Pitched ceilings of the chapel acted like a sounding board, capturing the rich harmonies and creating a sustained vibration in the room.

Then all was quiet again, except for the constant chatter of sparrows outside the window. The sweet aroma of candles filled the air. One brother dozed off and suddenly snored, waking himself. After ten days of almost nonstop activity and talking, I was immensely grateful for the shared solitude with God.

After an hour of silence, seven male voices joined in unison for a Pentecost hymn in lilting plainsong:

Come, Holy Ghost, Creator, come
    from thy bright heavenly throne,

Come, take possession of our souls,
and make them all thine own. . . .
Through thee may we the Father know,
through thee th' eternal Son.
And the Spirit of them both,
thrice-blessed Three in One.

After readings from Psalm 113 and Revelation 19, one voice led us in prayer: "We know that the Father is with us because of the Spirit he has given us. With this confidence, we turn to you in prayer: Father, send your Spirit into the church!"

There followed an open time of intercession, with concerns raised from the immediate community and from around the world. Following each petition, the brothers prayed in unison, "Father, send your Spirit into the church!"

A Pentecost Feast

From time to time, Franciscans step back from their austere and disciplined lives to celebrate a holy day of the church year. It was my good fortune to be with the friars for this feast of Pentecost. Brother Michael, Guardian (spiritual director) of the house, had laid out a long table in the dining room for a banquet. The robed friars directed me to a seat at the head of the table, between Brothers Andrew and Michael.

A prayer of thanksgiving signaled the beginning of a two-and-one-half-hour feast. With jovial informality, the friars all stood to reach across the table and dispense great servings of chicken, cabbage, potatoes, cooked carrots, gravy, white sauce, and home brew.

I learned that Brother Michael was my age (41), and I asked about his role as Guardian for the household.

The Guardian makes sure that each brother is progressing in his calling," he responded. "I'm the animator for the house-

The jovial friars all stood to fill their plates at the Pentecost feast.

hold; I help the brothers become what the Lord is calling them to be. I make sure they have time for prayer, and that structures of the community don't militate against a flourishing relationship with the Lord. If needed, I'm a reconciler between brothers.

I could imagine that reconciliation sometimes would be necessary. The friars included a former music student, a former navy man, and a grandfather. They ranged in age from late twenties to midseventies. The brothers came from Scotland, England, Switzerland, and Zambia. Brother Michael continued:

The Spirit of God enables people of many different backgrounds to live together. Our prayer life is most important in building community. We could function if we missed weekly "chapter" [administrative and decision-making] meetings for two months. But if we missed prayer for two months, the community would fall apart.

Communion has an important role in bringing about unity when there is destructive conflict, Brother Michael observed. "Celebrating eucharist is very difficult if you're not reconciled. Jesus said, 'First be reconciled to your brother or sister, and then come and offer your gift at the altar' [Matthew 5:24]."

Dealing with Conflict

Brother Michael's comments about reconciliation brought to my mind a flood of associations growing out of recent work I had done in conflict resolution. Jesus was often involved with conflict himself. He laid out specific instructions for how his followers should act when there is dispute or hurt in personal relationships:

> *You have heard that it was said to those of ancient times, "You shall not murder"; and "whoever murders shall be liable to judgment." But I say to you that if you are angry with a brother or sister, you will be liable to judgment; and if you insult a brother or sister, you will be liable to the council; and if you say, "You fool," you will be liable to the hell of fire. So when you are offering your gift at the altar, if you remember that your brother or sister has something against you, leave your gift there before the altar and go; first be reconciled to your brother or sister, and then come and offer your gift.* (Matthew 5:21-24)

Jesus does not say it's wrong to get angry. He simply reminds his followers that when we get angry, we move into a danger zone: God will review what we do with our anger ("you will be liable to judgment"). If we insult one another, then the matter also comes under review by the leadership of our faith community ("you will be liable to the council," literally, the "Sanhedrin," the governing body of the Jewish people in Jerusalem). If we re-sort to personal attack or humiliation by calling someone else a fool (literally, "empty-head"), then even our eternal spiritual des-tiny will be at stake ("you will be liable to the hell of fire").

The apostle Paul says "Be angry but do not sin; do not let the sun go down on your anger, and do not make room for the devil" (Ephesians 4:26-27). Both Jesus and Paul got angry at times. Both insist that we must deal promptly with such feelings. Both recognize that there is a spiritual dimension to conflict.

In Matthew 18:15-20, Jesus gives practical steps for what to do when another member of the church "sins (against you)":

1. Go and point out the fault when the two of you are alone.

2. If you are not listened to, take one or two others along with you.

3. If the member refuses to listen to them, tell it to the church.

4. If the offender refuses to listen even to the church, "let such a one be to you as a Gentile and a tax collector."

This is a brief outline for dealing with conflict, but behind it is great wisdom. There may be conflict between individuals, or a church member may see a fellow member committing sin not necessarily against the observer (Matthew 18:15, earliest texts; Galatians 6:1). Then it usually is best to go directly to the person in question and to state clearly where the hurt or sin lies. Jesus counsels us to keep the conflict private at this point.

A direct personal approach must be done in a non-accusato-ry way. The other person is most likely to hear us if we use "I" language to describe what we experienced or felt, such as, "I felt embarrassed when you made a negative comment about my work in front of the whole planning committee." Such wording is more likely to succeed than "you" language that might feel like an accusation, such as, "Why do you always try to embarrass me in front of the planning committee?"

If this private approach to conflict does not work, Jesus says we should go with one or two other members of the church to speak with the individual in question. It's important not to invite only people who already side with me. That might make the other individual feel defensive and angry. The extra "witnesses" must be people trusted and respected by both parties in the conflict. Paul calls for those who "have received the Spirit" to "restore such a one in a spirit of gentleness" (Galatians 6:1-2).

If this step bears no fruit, then the issue must in one way or another come to the attention of the congregation. Individuals with hurt or concern can begin this step by talking the matter over with the minister and the pastoral care team or the church council.

Finally, if the person who did wrong will not listen even to the whole church, then they shall be put out of full fellowship with the congregation. Even in this sad circumstance, however, believers must be loving. Jesus showed kindness and offered forgiveness to Gentiles and tax collectors! He even ate with them (Matthew 9:10; Luke 5:29; 19:5-7).

Reconciliation both within and beyond the faith community is Holy Spirit work. At the end of his discussion about steps for dealing with conflict, Jesus says, "Where two or three are gathered in my name, I am there among them" (Matthew 18:20). Jesus is uniquely present through his Spirit when his followers work to make peace.

When Jesus first met his disciples after the resurrection, he brought together peacemaking, the Holy Spirit, and mission almost in one breath: "Peace be with you. As the Father has sent me, so I send you. . . . Receive the Holy Spirit. If you forgive the sins of any, they are forgiven them" (John 20:21-23).

Prayer Is About Everything That Life Can Offer

With ninety minutes of worship still fresh on my mind, I asked Brother Michael what he has learned about prayer.

> Sometimes I pray, and the Lord is there. Other times I say, "Lord, why do you stand afar off?" Prayer is about everything that life can offer: joy, dryness, or the feeling that a relationship isn't going anywhere. Sometimes prayer is ecstatic, but to stay there is not possible. If you try to sustain euphoria, prayer becomes an unreal relationship.
>
> Spiritual growth is like the ebb and flow of a marriage; a sudden or dramatic conversion needs a time of rooting. Ecstatic experience has to come down to a quieter, day-to-day level that can be sustained. Even Jesus struggled in Gethsemane and felt abandoned on the cross. Mary had a very different experience standing at the foot of the cross than she did when the angel announced Jesus' birth.

At this point Brother Peter noted that the Psalms feature large in the daily cycle of worship followed by the friars. "The Psalms are very human," he said. "They aren't always nice, but they reflect feelings we may really need to express."

Brother Peter's comment about the Psalms was helpful; the Psalms register a wide range of human emotions: joy, fear, anger, doubt, even hatred. The Psalms do not teach us to doubt or to hate. They simply provide a model of how we bring such feelings to God: honestly, openly, with nothing to hide. God's Spirit can begin to change us as when we are so free in prayer.

How does Brother Michael structure his times of silent prayer?

> Prayer is meditative. It does not mean making a shopping list. Usually I begin by acknowledging God's presence and acknowledging my own presence. I normally focus on a line

from a Psalm or a hymn, such as "Come, Holy Spirit." Or I meditate on one of the powerful images from the writings of the apostle Paul, such as, "He is the image of the invisible God" (Colossians 1:15).

Brother Michael, Guardian of the Franciscan community at Canterbury

Michael acknowledged that daily prayer sometimes can become mundane and barren. "Prayer must be sustained by commitment, not by heady experience," he said.

Brother Michael offered the following counsel for new believers:

Never allow your growing relationship with God to be divorced from the real world. Bring anger, doubt, and joy into your prayers. Allow the Lord to take over every area of your life. Long after you become a Christian, there still will be unresolved issues.

You may want to deny that some issues are unresolved

because you think you are a new creation. Unresolved issues among the friars, for example, may include matters related to chastity or obedience. We regularly have to ask, Are we prepared to follow in the footsteps of Christ? We are likely to want power and control. Will we allow Jesus to be Lord and Master?

Members of the Capuchin order are called "Friars Minor" (lesser brothers), Michael explained. "We are lesser brothers before each other and before the world," he said, "and that is hard. It's natural to want to be powerful. That's an issue for every Christian. We all are called to fidelity and obedience."

I asked Brother Michael if he ever meets former classmates from university, with their families and status and good jobs, and says to himself, "What if I had done that?"

He laughed. "I certainly do—and then I say, 'Thank God!' Some of them are divorced, and most don't have nearly as rich a life as I have had."

During the entire meal, a cacophony of conversations and laughter filled the room. The brothers were giving as much attention to fellowship as to food. At last it was time for dessert. Out came cake, followed by Stilton cheese, crackers, and coffee. Then we all stood for the standard provincial prayer used after a meal by Franciscans in the United Kingdom:

Leader: Give thanks to the Lord, for he is good.
All: He provides for all living creatures. Glory be
to the Father.
Leader: We thank you, Lord, for the gifts we have received.
Make us generous to those in want, and always grateful
for what you have given us. Through Christ our Lord.
Amen.

Epilogue

Brother Damon visited the London Mennonite Centre a few months after he had walked with Ellen and me into Canterbury. He had just completed a two-week pilgrimage of his own, in Ireland.

In contrast to my rather cushy approach of staying in bed-and-breakfast lodging, Brother Damon spent nights as a homeless person in a sleeping bag, in the doorways of churches and other public buildings. He wore jeans and sneakers instead of a friar's habit, and carried only £75 ($115) for the entire trip. One night at 2:00 a.m. he was awakened and questioned by the police.

He described all this to me in his usual jovial manner, and then laughed at the weather he endured. "It rained eleven out of thirteen days. The first four days, I sang songs to 'Sister Rain,' like St. Francis did. Then on the fifth morning, I said, 'No, not rain again! So much for Sister Rain. Francis was a nutter! Maybe he could sing about rain in balmy, Mediterranean Italy—but this is a cold week in Ireland. I want some sun!' "

I took Brother Damon into the Mennonite Centre library and showed him a section of books related to Anabaptism. "You might be interested in this," I said, as I pulled off the shelf a great tome called *Martyrs Mirror*. It's a seventeenth-century book with stories of thousands of Christian martyrs, especially featuring those from the sixteenth-century Anabaptist movement.

I set the book down, and it fell open to a page that included an engraving. "What's this?" Brother Damon asked with interest, as he leaned down to examine the engraving and read the text. "It's a picture of an Anabaptist being interrogated by a friar!" he said with alarm, and read further. "Oh no—it's a *Franciscan* friar!"

The story ended with the Anabaptist being executed. Brother Damon threw his hands into the air. "Forgive me, forgive me, my brother! How could a Franciscan do that to an Anabaptist?"

Then, despite the horror of the story, we both broke into

laughter. That expressed our relief and gratitude that we live in a time when Christians of differing traditions can love and learn from each other rather than try to change one another by hatred or force.

Prayer

Lord, in the life and death of Jesus, you showed how deeply you care about every woman, man, and child. Thank you for extending that love to me in compassion, forgiveness, and healing. Teach me to value other people as you value me. Help me to be like Jesus in how I deal with conflict—to be direct, honest, and loving, even when I hurt. Thank you for a Christian community of sisters and brothers who provide counsel, encouragement, and guidance. Let your Spirit fill me with grace and strength to be a joyful participant in the church and in your kingdom. Amen.

For Reflection

1. What evidence do you see that society values or does not value individuals? What people did Jesus especially seek out to affirm and love?

2. What messages do you receive from the media or from elsewhere in society about the role and significance of sexuality? How do these expectations differ from what Jesus taught for his followers?

3. Think of a time recently when you had a conflict with a friend, family member, or church member. How did you deal with the conflict? What might you change about your response in view of New Testament teaching about conflict?

4. Who in your personal life or faith community plays the role of "guardian" and restorer? In what ways do you find mutual accountability and encouragement in the church?

12

Travel with Other Pilgrims

Monday, May 27
Canterbury to Nonington (9 miles)
Hosts: Members of the Bruderhof

Wealth or power can destroy spiritual vitality by allowing us to rely on ourselves rather than God • The privilege of following Jesus is the greatest joy we can know • We aren't made to be solo Christians • God calls all believers to some form of community • Being in community is difficult and always brings conflict • People of all ages and abilities are important to the faith community • Following Jesus means finding practical ways to respond to needs of the world.

Satisfied with the Basics

Morning prayers at the friary were from 7:15 to 8:15 a.m., with the first half hour in silence. The brothers, I noticed, all returned to the same chairs they had used the evening before. There is a certain amount of routine that many people find valuable in prayer, a familiar pattern that reduces unnecessary decisions, freeing the mind to focus on God.

Being new to the brothers' prayer books and songbooks, I became disoriented during the liturgy with the sequence of readings and texts. More than once Brother Loarne, seated beside me, leaned over to point me to the right page.

I spent the silent time thanking God for the rich experiences

I'd had over the previous ten days. Could it be only ten days? By now, I felt completely removed from the daily routine of telephone, computer, doorbell, deadlines, speaking engagements, and family responsibilities. It seemed I had been walking for months and had become a different person.

Now I was more aware of God, unencumbered by excess baggage, and satisfied with the basics of clothing, shelter, food, and companionship. I was more pilgrim than tourist. What would it be like to go back to normal life? I didn't want my pilgrimage to end, and I resolved that it would not. I may have to go back to London the next day, but I would take into the city some of the sensitivity to God and awareness of myself that had developed on the Pilgrims' Way.

A tiny figurine of St. Francis with his arms around the dying Christ

" 'Come and have breakfast'—as our Lord said to his disciples!" It was Brother Damon speaking at the end of morning prayers, with characteristic humor. Later I confirmed that the breakfast invitation was a direct quote from Jesus as host and apparently as cook (John 21:9-12)!

In contrast to dinner the previous night, breakfast was simple: oatmeal, toast, coffee, and tea. The brothers bid me a warm farewell, then hurried out in many directions to their various places of work and study.

Brother Damon lingered behind, and as I set out from the friary, he pressed into my hand a tiny figurine. It portrays Francis of Assisi standing at the foot of the cross, with his arms around the dying Christ. "This represents the solidarity Francis expressed with the sufferings of Jesus, " Brother Damon said. "Francis was determined to reach out to Christ in the suffering of the world."

Two Major Streams of Christian Heritage

At the eastern edge of Canterbury, I stopped by the ruins of St. Augustine's Abbey, a monastery founded in A.D. 598. An Italian monk by that name (not the better-known fourth-century church father) arrived to bring Christianity to Britain.

Christianity had been known centuries earlier when Britain was under Roman rule, but it largely died out in southeastern England after the fall of the Roman empire. Under pressure from pagan invaders, the practice of Christian faith had been pushed westward to Wales, Ireland, and the islands of Scotland. Late in the sixth century, Augustine was sent from Rome to establish a base for the Catholic Church at Canterbury, with the support of a local king.

While he and others sought to evangelize Britain from the east, indigenous Christians in western parts of the British Isles were developing a different strain of the faith. It came to be known as Celtic Christianity.

Ruins of St. Augustine's Abbey at Canterbury

I feel a kinship with the Celtic expression of Christian faith that flourished in the British Isles before Roman Catholicism came to dominate the region in the sixth century. Celtic society was not hierarchical and was decentralized, in contrast to the class-conscious and male-dominated church of Rome. Celtic Christianity emphasized praying communities rather than weighty doctrinal books.

From places such as tiny Iona Island in western Scotland, Celtic monks launched a missionary movement that sent wandering evangelists across Britain and Europe. People in this branch of the Christian family used women in leadership, viewed the world as basically good, did not possess great political or military power, and developed a simple style of prayer that reflected a sensitivity to the rhythms of country life:

O great God, aid Thou my soul
With the aiding of Thine own mercy;
Even as I clothe my body with wool,
Cover Thou my soul with the shadow of Thy wing.

Help me to avoid every sin,
And the source of every sin to forsake;
And as the mist scatters on the crest of the hills,
May each ill haze clear from my soul, O God.[1]

That prayer is one of thousands written down a century ago among Celtic people in the Highlands and Islands of Scotland. The Celtic movement lost institutional power in the seventh century when the Catholic Church extended its influence over large parts of Britain. Yet vestiges of this gentle and earthy expression of Christianity survived in isolated islands and mountain hamlets.

I am drawn to Christian movements that don't rely on great power, wealth, or influence. The most exciting Christians I've met have been those "at the edge," people who by circumstance or by choice live out the gospel in such a way that they have to depend on God and the faith community rather than their social status or political clout.

From the start of the Christian church, there have been committed disciples of Jesus in all social and economic levels of society. But wealthy or socially prominent Christians must be aware that such comfort can destroy spiritual vitality by allowing us to rely on ourselves rather than God.

Tears of Gratitude and Fatigue

After so many days of intensive interaction with others, it was wonderful to spend Monday walking alone. Just outside Canterbury, I walked through orchards in full, glorious blossom. Corn seedlings nudged up through wet soil. The day had started cloudy, but now the sun broke through to warm my body and soul. I stopped and ate my sandwiches at the village of Patrixbourne, in the graveyard of an old church mentioned in the eleventh-century *Domesday Book*. I realized that my Achilles tendons still hurt, and my legs still ached.

In early afternoon, the intensity of the last two weeks swept over me. I found myself walking several miles with tears streaming down my cheeks. Part of that emotion was fatigue: the combination of daily physical effort and intense focus on conversation had taken a lot out of me. Now I was alone, and had no need to contain whatever welled up within.

I was so full of gratitude for knowing Jesus that I could not find words, and tears expressed that gratitude better than spoken prayer. The privilege of following Jesus seemed more precious than anything I have ever known. Day after day on this walk, I had been with people who deeply longed to know God, and their experiences had changed me. How could I thank God for taking me on a journey that really *means* something, both on the Pilgrims' Way and in life?

A Place Where Brothers and Sisters Live

The Pilgrims' Way ended at Canterbury. I now was on a branch of the North Downs Way that carries on to the English Channel. Near Aylesham I left the main walking route and headed north across fields and farms to the Beech Grove Bruderhof community, at the village of Nonington.

Christians in the Bruderhof movement relinquish all personal possessions, after an extended test period of living at the community. They live as an intergenerational community. Knowing that members of the Bruderhof live simply, I was a bit startled to see the grand (though somewhat abandoned-looking) country estate house they had recently acquired. By the gate a handmade wooden sign read:

Bruderhof means "a place where brothers live." We are a fellowship of families and single people who share all things in common and seek together to live a life based on the gospel of Jesus, as the early Christians did.

Eberhard Arnold and others founded this Christian communal group in Germany in 1920. Also known as the Society of Brothers, these believers were persecuted during Hitler's totalitarian regime and were expelled from Germany in 1937. Bruderhof Communities have been established in England, Paraguay (now closed), and the United States. For twenty-five years there has been a thriving community at Robertsbridge in southern England. Some three hundred Christians live there and welcome visits from anyone who seeks to know Jesus.

The Nonington group was less than a year old when I visited, still struggling to establish a factory enterprise that will enable them to be financially self-sustaining. They had purchased the grounds of a defunct college. The community had a massive job on their hands, repairing and renovating the halls, dormitories, gymnasium, and estate house. When I visited, the new Bruderhof had only eighty residents, but they hoped to expand to three hundred.

Two young women in Bruderhof attire (long skirts and head scarfs) were walking across the grounds, and greeted me warmly. They took me into the dining hall in a smaller building beyond the abandoned estate house. There members of the community were finishing an afternoon tea break. I knew some of the members since I had met them at the other Bruderhof in England.

Then I was shown to a simple bedroom in the basement. A sign on the door read, "Welcome, dear Nelson." Flowers and a small bowl of fruit were on a table by my bed.

Not Made to Be Solo Christians

At 7:00 p.m. the community assembled for dinner at long tables in the dining hall. The smallest children were in care elsewhere while the rest of the members ate. We sang a quaint folk song to a German melody, then had a brief prayer. Young men brought in steaming platters of food. Everyone ate in silence while a voice on the public address system read from a book.

I have been at several Bruderhof meals. The readings have varied from letters to novels. The goal is to read something that will nurture people of all ages. On this occasion the book was a history of Bruderhof experiences in South America.

Near the end of the meal, someone brought a microphone to me, and asked me to make a few comments while the others finished eating. I briefly described whom I had walked with, then offered the following observations about those fellow pilgrims:

1. People who risk the most for God have the most compelling things to say.

2. Those who pray often and know the Scriptures seem to have the deepest spiritual wells.

3. We aren't made to be solo Christians. We need other wayfarers by our side.

4. Following Jesus might exact a high price in terms of success, safety, and security.

5. Humble and unpretentious people sometimes have the greatest wisdom.

6. There are deeply committed followers of Jesus in many Christian traditions.

7. Sometimes we look like fools for taking Jesus seriously.

8. There may be passages of pain in following Jesus, but also abiding joy.

Members of the Bruderhof sharing a common meal

After the meal the young men efficiently washed dishes. Then all adults assembled for a "Brotherhood Meeting," a regular gathering where members weigh issues and make community decisions. Not being a member, I could not participate. A thirty-five-year-old father named Micha Mathis invited me to his apartment instead. As we visited, he held his infant daughter and talked about his experience of living in community.

Finding Life in Community

"God calls all of his people to *some* form of community," began Micha Mathis. "I can't imagine being a Christian hermit." He noted that the Bruderhof, where all possessions are held in common, has some similarities to communism.

> However, communism doesn't work very well as a political ideology because it leaves out God. Without God, the notion that material goods should be distributed "to each according to their need" quickly becomes selfish.

The Bruderhof people base their economic and communal practices on the model of the early church at Jerusalem after Pentecost. More than three thousand believers shared a common life:

> *They devoted themselves to the apostles' teaching and fellowship, to the breaking of bread and the prayers.*
> *Awe came upon everyone, because many wonders and signs were being done by the apostles. All who believed were together and had all things in common; they would sell their possessions and goods and distribute the proceeds to all, as any had need. Day by day, as they spent much time together in the temple, they broke bread at home and ate their food with glad and generous hearts, praising God and having the goodwill of all the people. And day by day the Lord added to their number those who were being saved.* (Acts 2:42-47; cf. 4:32-35)

Micha Mathis and his infant daughter

Micha said he was raised in a Bruderhof, but between the ages of nineteen and twenty-five he lived outside the community. He went to university, then lived in Philadelphia, Pennsylvania, working with Mennonites in a home-repair project for the very poor. "It was a rough part of the city. I got into homes where there was no electricity, no running water, no sewer."

After that experience, Micha went to Los Angeles and worked among the poor with another Christian ministry. "That was a war zone. We often heard gunfire at night," he recalled.

Those experiences of urban violence and poverty made a deep impression on Micha, and drew him back toward intentional Christian community. "In the inner city I felt like I was putting a Band-Aid on a huge wound. What we were offering was not adequate to the needs. I worked with children, teaching Bible stories. I did maintenance projects, and took urban kids on hikes into the countryside."

What the city needed, Micha decided, was a new way for people to relate to each other in community. He was part of a small intentional Christian community, but it did not work well.

> We could sing and pray and shout together, but we could not get along in the day-to-day operation of the projects. I began to have a new appreciation for what people of the Bruderhof have accomplished and learned. It is possible for Christians to live in a new society. Here my children have no contact with drugs, with the violence of television, or with child abuse.

Micha's description of the Bruderhof made it sound like an ideal place, but he was quick to acknowledge their own struggles.

> We regularly have people come to the Bruderhof and say this is what they're looking for. They are all ready to give up

everything and join. In a week or two, they realize that Bruderhof members have problems, that we aren't spiritual giants! Then the new people start missing their football matches and their independence. For the first three days, they say, "This place is paradise." Then in a week or two, they say, "This place is hell!"

Micha laughed, but he was making a serious point. "Following Christ costs, but that is true fulfillment. Go shopping for pearls. Find and invest in the one worth the most" (Matthew 13:45-46).

Ordinary Saints and Redeemed Sinners

Christian community in any form, whether the Bruderhof or a local congregation, is made up of ordinary saints and redeemed sinners. They do not perfectly reflect the grace of God. This especially comes to light when there is conflict—a common experience in any Christian church or community. Micha shared:

It's really a gift to be able to resolve conflicts every day between me and my brothers. In many churches, people sweep conflicts under the carpet and try to act happy together. When you live together as we do, you have to sort out your problems. All of our little idiosyncrasies become obvious. If we weren't at the Bruderhof for the right reasons, those little things would really blow up. You can't just be here for your own security and happiness. That's not enough; it has to be for God.

Group decisions at the Bruderhof are made on the basis of absolute unity, not by majority vote. "It often happens that most brothers and sisters agree on a given issue, but one or two don't," Micha said. "If we can't come to unity, then we'll leave that issue for a while, and come back to it later. It's happened already that the ninety-nine percent then change their mind and agree with the one percent."

I asked Micha if he doesn't ever simply wish to run his own life again. He responded thoughtfully,

> For a while I lived alone at the edge of London. I bicycled all over southern England, and took vacations when I wanted. I found it is hollow and empty to do your own thing. It's joyful and fulfilling to do God's will. When I moved back to the Bruderhof, the community decided to send me to work with one of our communities in the United States. Just before I left, the other single young men of the Bruderhof took me out early in the morning to watch the sun rise. It was rainy, cloudy, and miserable—but the fellowship was deep and satisfying.

A City Set on a Hill

Life-giving community is not something that can happen just with good intentions, Micha insisted. "Our own salvation as individuals has to be the starting point for community. But God saves us *to do his will*. There's something much greater that God wants for us than just our individual salvation."

Part of what God wants is to create a faith community in which every member is deeply valued. "My grandmother is eighty-one," Micha continued. "Every day she still goes to work in the archives of the Bruderhof. She has a role. She also helps look after babies and is still needed by the community. We have no concept of retirement here. We're in it to the end. Everyone has a place."

My reading from the Psalms that day, playful in its description of community, kept coming to mind as Micha and I spoke:

How very good and pleasant it is
when kindred live together in unity!
It is like the precious oil on the head,
running down upon the beard,
on the beard of Aaron,
running down over the collar of his robes.
It is like the dew of Hermon,
which falls on the mountains of Zion.
For there the Lord ordained his blessing,
life forevermore. (Psalm 133:1-3)

Micha described how young children at the Bruderhof come around to the workshop and other places of activity, and bring cookies for the adults. "We don't put old people in homes and kids in a daycare. Instead, we experience life together. We've given up ourselves and want to be a 'city built on a hill' " (Matthew 5:14). However, Micha was quick to add that the Bruderhof is far from perfect.

We are not an ideal group of Christians, living exemplary lives in front of the world. But the Holy Spirit does break in through our weaknesses to the glory of God. The kingdom of God can take practical form here and now—if people are really gathered in Jesus' name, if they're not just clapping each other on the back and trying to be happy. If we don't allow the Holy Spirit into our lives, something else will take control.

One sign of the Holy Spirit, Micha said, is when Christians begin to break away from being controlled by money and material possessions. "When the Spirit hit the church in the book of Acts, the believers began to share. How can the love of Christ be in the church if some members are in need and others have wealth?"

Mark and Sue Greenyer's daughter at the breakfast table

The Bruderhof model of living together with all things in common is not the only biblical way for Christians to relate to one another. Nevertheless, there is joy and freedom in the disciplined way of life that these people have rediscovered.

Back to a Jaded City

Family units at the Bruderhof each have their own apartments and have at least one meal by themselves every day. Single people each relate to a particular family, so they don't eat alone. I was warmly welcomed into the home of Mark and Sue

Greenyer and their children for a simple breakfast on Tuesday morning.

There was work to be done at the Bruderhof, and I had an 8:27 a.m. train to catch several miles away. Mark offered me a ride. For the first time on my pilgrimage, I crawled into a car. After almost two weeks of seeing the world at walking speed, the car seemed to race across the countryside.

At midmorning my train came to a stop at bustling Victoria Station in London. Straight out the window, a billboard advertising cut-rate airline seats for overseas flights yelled, "Vote with your backside." Yes, I definitely was back in a jaded city!

I threaded my way through a teeming throng of travelers, shoulder-to-shoulder people from every nation on earth, it seemed. While I waited in line to buy a ticket to the Underground trains, there was a tap on my shoulder. A young man about age twenty, with earnest eyes and long black hair, said with a foreign accent, "Can you spare some change?" I said no—and then began to wonder what Jesus meant by telling us to be the salt of the earth.

With ticket in hand, I approached the young man and engaged him in conversation. He was from Rome and came to London five months earlier to study English. He could not get a job, was out of money, and needed lunch. I had no way to verify the story, but he looked defeated, and I gave him a pound coin. His face lit up, and he said with a smile, "You saved me today."

The Underground train was so crowded that, even though I was blessed to have a seat for the brief ride, another traveler stood with a rucksack poking into my face. I got off the train at Highgate and took the long escalator ride to ground level. Two hundred commercial posters assaulted my senses from both sides of the moving stairway.

Just outside the Underground station, I passed a grove of trees where several local homeless men live in makeshift shacks. Coming down toward the station was Kyra, a sixteen-year-old school-girl who was with my daughter Laura six months earlier. That was the time Laura was attacked on the street for no apparent reason by a middle-aged man. Laura was not hurt, but I remembered the anger, fear, and reflex to get even that our family felt that week.

Awaiting a New City

Perhaps it was appropriate for my pilgrimage to end in a great city. That is how the long story of God's dealings with humanity ends in the Bible. The book of Revelation, which uses vivid poetry to describe the sufferings of a world full of violence and greed, ends with the glorious vision of a New Jerusalem:

> *Then I saw a new heaven and a new earth; for the first heaven and the first earth had passed away, and the sea was no more. And I saw the holy city, the new Jerusalem, coming down out of heaven from God, prepared as a bride adorned for her husband. And I heard a loud voice from the throne saying,*
> *"See, the home of God is among mortals.*
> *He will dwell with them as their God;*
> *they will be his peoples,*
> *and God himself will be with them;*
> *he will wipe every tear from their eyes.*
> *Death will be no more;*
> *mourning and crying and pain will be no more,*
> *for the first things have passed away."*
> *And the one who was seated on the throne said, "See, I am making all things new." Also he said, "Write this, for these words are trustworthy and true." Then he said to me, "It is done! I am the Alpha and the Omega, the beginning and the end. To the thirsty I will give water as a gift from the spring of the water of life. Those who conquer will inherit these things, and I will be their God and they will be my children. (Revelation 21:1-7)*

Most Christians understand this vision as a preview of what will happen at the end of time, when Jesus returns to bring final liberation from sin, suffering, and death. If God in the end will make a "new heaven and a new earth," then even the most dire situations of misery or evil will someday be made right.

However, the image in Revelation 21 doesn't seem to be so much one of God *replacing* one world with another, but rather one of God *restoring* creation to what it was meant to be. Some day God again will dwell among mortals in the same free fellowship that Adam and Eve knew in the Garden of Eden. God is the "Alpha and Omega" (the "*A* to *Z*"), the "beginning and the end."

Imagery of a New Jerusalem coming down to earth from heaven apparently is John's way of saying, "Your will be done on earth as it is in heaven." Some day the human family will be restored to harmony and wholeness, and it will require the intervention of God to make that complete.

In the meantime, though, people who know the love of Jesus already experience a foretaste of what it will be like when God restores all of creation. In Spirit-filled congregations and communities the world over, men and women find their individual and communal lives made new.

People who know the risen Christ have power to live by the constitution of "the city that is to come" (Hebrews 13:14). This puts into tangible form the practice of the kingdom of God today. Hence, it makes sense for John the Seer to claim that this city is already in the process of "coming" (Revelation 3:12; 21:2, 12).

Words of Hope and Life

It was time for noon prayers when I arrived at the London Mennonite Centre. I joined staff and household members around a single candle in the chapel. The worship leader began to read from the Sermon on the Mount, simple words of life that are a manifesto of the kingdom of God (Matthew 5:3-10):

Blessed are the poor in spirit,
   for theirs is the kingdom of heaven.
Blessed are those who mourn,
   for they will be comforted.
Blessed are the meek,
   for they will inherit the earth.
Blessed are those who hunger and thirst for justice,
   for they will be filled.
Blessed are the merciful,
   for they will receive mercy.
Blessed are the pure in heart,
   for they will see God.
Blessed are the peacemakers,
   for they will be called children of God.
Blessed are those who are persecuted for righteousness' sake,
   for theirs is the kingdom of heaven.

In the silence that followed, I reflected on what my pilgrimage meant now that I was back in the city. Here consumerism, human need, and even violence are all too familiar. In the lives of a dozen or more pilgrims, with all their joy and pain and insight, I had met the risen Christ. I had walked with Jesus on the Pilgrims' Way. Now I had to decide what day-to-day difference my walk with Jesus would make.

Those twelve days of walking and talking about discipleship were some of the richest of my life, but they required discipline and focus. I had a destination and a purpose for the walk. Now I wanted the same for my daily life. My destination as a Christian is the kingdom of God—not only a heavenly place to live after I die, but a down-to-earth family of sisters and brothers the world over, believers who acknowledge Jesus as Lord.

My purpose as a Christian is to live by the joy and the expectations of that kingdom, and to invite others to do the same. Jesus is both pioneer and fellow pilgrim on this journey into the kingdom, showing me in practical terms how to live a changed life.

I will not walk this pilgrimage alone. Everywhere I go, I will seek out others going in the same direction. We will carry one another's burdens, worship together, work side by side for justice, and invite other travelers to know our Lord. This journey will grow out of hope and gratitude, not out of guilt or duty.

We will laugh and cry and pray together, and draw our strength from the Spirit of Jesus among us. We will tell stories of God's faithfulness. We will take delight in crossing barriers of race, class, nationality, and gender. This is life lived fully. I cannot imagine ever seeking a different destination.

I will not walk this way simply for my own spiritual or emotional fulfillment, but will give my best energies to being an ambassador of hope in a broken world. Jesus walked all the way to Jerusalem to lay down his life for me. Just the same way, I will walk wherever God calls me to show love to those who are alone, hungry, or afraid.

I will work for peace between individuals and peace between nations. I will speak the love of Jesus whenever possible. I will live for the day when Jesus returns to complete for all creation the process of restoration he already has begun in the humble lives of ordinary people like you and me.

Prayer

Creator God, I yearn to be at home with people who know you and who share extravagant hope in your plans for the future. I want to see the big picture of where history is headed, so that I have confidence to be faithful to you even in hard circumstances. The call to follow Jesus is exhilarating, liberating, and difficult. I need to walk the way of Jesus with others who know the joy of your presence, the freedom of your forgiveness, and the power of your Spirit. May your kingdom come, may your will be done in my life as it is in heaven. Come, Lord Jesus! Amen.

For Reflection

1. Do you know Christian individuals or groups who live "at the edge" of society, pushed to the margins for economic, social, or political reasons? Are such people more or less likely to take seriously the teachings of Jesus?

2. Do you have any experience with economic sharing or community living? If so, what were the joys or headaches of that kind of living? If not, what small or large steps might you be willing to take in that direction? Would you consider helping form a plan at your church to share financially with members in need?

3. What physical or social needs do you see in your home area? Within your church community? In what ways might you or your church address these needs?

4. What difference does it make to you now to know that some day God will bring all of creation into peace and harmony?

Tips for Walking the Pilgrims' Way

The Pilgrims' Way is an ancient footpath that goes across southern England from Winchester Cathedral to Canterbury Cathedral, mostly on a wooded ridge called the North Downs. The North Downs Way as a footpath was officially opened in 1978. It mostly coincides with the Pilgrims' Way, 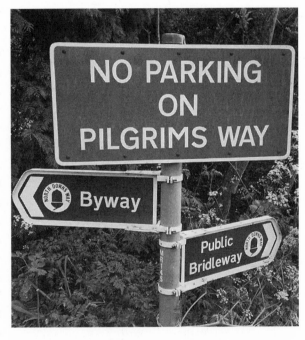 but leads into nearby scenic areas when the Pilgrims' Way goes through an urban or industrial stretch.

Instead of starting at Winchester, the North Downs Way begins twenty-eight miles east, at Farnham (where I began my walk for this book). The North Downs Way detours sharply north where it crosses the River Medway near Rochester. Otherwise it always coincides with or stays close to the old path. The Pilgrims'

Way ends at Canterbury, and the North Downs Way continues on to the coast at Dover.

I found two books especially helpful in planning:

• Christopher John Wright, *A Guide to the Pilgrims' Way and North Downs Way,* A Constable Guide, 4th edition (Constable & Co. Ltd. [3 The Lanchesters, 162 Fulham Rd., London W6 9ER, U.K.], 1993). The colorful text includes local history and folklore. Its maps need to be supplemented either with the Curtis book (below) or with Ordnance Survey maps.

• Neil Curtis, *North Downs Way,* A National Trail Guide (Aurum Press [10 Museum St., London WC1A 1JS, U.K.], 1992). This book includes the Ordnance Survey maps required for the North Downs Way, but does not include the Pilgrims' Way from Winchester to Farnham.

Ordnance Survey maps are beautifully detailed, on a scale of 1:50,000 (1 ¼ inch to 1 mile). They are available in bookstores throughout the United Kingdom (or from Dept. IC, Ordnance Survey, Romsey Rd., Maybush, Southampton SO9 4DH, U.K.).

For walking the entire Pilgrims' Way, it would be necessary to acquire maps number 185 to 189. Relevant sections for the North Downs Way are included in the Curtis book (above). Transparent map carriers, with a cord for around the neck, are available from outdoor sports shops throughout the United Kingdom.

For tips on walking in the United Kingdom and for information on lodging, visit the following website:

www.visitbritain.com

You may wish to contact—

British Tourist Authority
12 Regent St.
Piccadilly Circus, London SW1Y 4PQ, U.K.
Telephone: 0181-846-9000 (see note below on dialing)
Fax: 0181-563-3276 (to dial either number from outside
    the U.K., omit the initial 0)

Three figures walking on the Pilgrims' Way: Laura, Ellen, and Andrea Kraybill

In the United States contact the website or—
British Tourist Authority
551 5th Ave., 7th Floor
New York, New York 10176-0799
Telephone: 800-462-2748 (or 212-986-2200)

Notes

Chapter 3: Choose the Better Part
1. Arthur P. Boers, *Builder,* May 1991, 53.
2. Thieleman J. van Braght, *Martyrs Mirror,* trans. Joseph F. Sohm from the 1660 Dutch original, third English edition (Scottdale, Pa.: Herald Press, 1938), 977-979.

Chapter 6: Turn the World Upside Down
1. "Noel" is pronounced as one syllable, rhyming with "bowl."

Chapter 7: Turn the World Upside Down
1. "Arfon" is pronounced "AR-von."

Chapter 12: Travel with Other Pilgrims
1. From a prayer entitled "Thanksgiving," in *Carmina Galelica,* III:3, as quoted by Esther de Waal, *The Celtic Vision: Prayers and Blessings from the Outer Hebrides* (London: Darton, Longman & Todd, 1988), 39.

The Author

Born and raised on a Mennonite farm in Pennsylvania, J. Nelson Kraybill has studied and worked in Costa Rica, Spain, Puerto Rico, and England. He prepared for the ministry at Princeton Theological Seminary and was pastor at a Mennonite congregation in Vermont.

After completing a Ph.D. in New Testament at Union Theological Seminary in Virginia, he served for five years as Programme Director at the London Mennonite Centre in England. He was cofounder of the Bridge Builders Mediation Service in London, and was coeditor of the magazine *Anabaptism Today*.

Kraybill is the author of *Imperial Cult and Commerce in John's Apocalypse*, a scholarly study of the book of Revelation. In 1997 he began serving as president of Associated Mennonite Biblical Seminary, Elkhart, Indiana.

Nelson is married to Ellen Graber, a physical therapist and musician. Together they wrote *Miscarriage: A Quiet Grief*. They have two daughters and worship at Prairie Street Mennonite Church, in Elkhart.